THE NINE LIFE CAT

THE NINE LIFE CAT

BRITAIN'S LEADING CAT EXPERT EXPLAINS
THE SECRETS OF HOW TO GIVE YOUR CAT A
LONGER, HEALTHIER, HAPPIER LIFE.

CLAIRE BESSANT
AND BRADLEY VINER

JOHN BLAKE

Published by Metro Publishing Ltd
3 Bramber Court
2 Bramber Road
London W14 9PB, England

First published in 2003

ISBN 1 843580 79 9

British Library Cataloguing-in-Publication Data: A catalogue
record for this book is available from the British Library.

Design by www.envydesign.co.uk

Printed in Great Britain by Creative Print and Design
(Wales), Ebbw Vale, Gwent

1 3 5 7 9 10 8 6 4 2

Papers used by Metro Publishing Ltd are natural,
recyclable products made from wood grown in sustainable forests.
The manufacturing processes conform to the environmental
regulations of the country of origin.

To old cats and their owners everywhere

To Dillon, my first and dearest cat who taught me a lot of what
I know about elderly cats – *Bradley*

For Steve, Sinead, Lucy, Georgia and Sorcha

Acknowledgements

With many thanks to our families for their patience in the preparation of this book.

Thanks to Karen Bessant for her help with the *Old Cat Survey*. *Cat World* and *Bristol Evening Post* readers made a large contribution with helpful facts, figures and stories of their own old cats. Thanks, too, to Sarah Hartwell and all the other FAB members who let us use their wonderful letters about their old cat experiences.

While every effort has been made to clear copyright for Alexander Gray's 'On a cat ageing', this has not proved possible. However, the publisher would like to hear from the copyright holder for any future edition.

Contents

4. A-Z of Aged Afflictions 47

5. Feline Cuisine 77

6. Best Behaviour 87

7. Old Friends 113

8. Lap of Luxury 139

9. Letting go and Starting Over 163

Introduction

Not so very long ago cats lived alongside us rather than with us. They came and went as they pleased, hunted for a portion of their food and were sometimes lucky enough to get some scraps from the table and a warm spot on the hearth. We didn't really know how old our cats were or how long they lived. If they survived disease, reproduction and accident they were doing well.

How things have changed for most pet cats. These days cats are very much members of the family, acknowledged as important parts of our lives and given the best seat next to the fire (or more likely the radiator), neutered and cared for with great affection. Now we do know how long our cats are living and much more about their veterinary care. Most do not have to undergo the rigours of sexual competition and reproduction and are given the best in terms of food and comfort.

We are learning what affects how long our cats live and have the tools to influence this. For example, vaccinations greatly reduce the number of cats suffering from infectious diseases; proper nutrition and parasite control also contribute to a healthier life and, of course, veterinary care has changed drastically. Another factor is that owners are now demanding that their cats get the highest-quality care and that the information and products available in the canine world are also there for cats. Conditions which would previously have been lumped together and excused as 'old age' are now being diagnosed and also successfully treated. Between owners and vets the care available to our cats has changed beyond recognition in the past 50 years.

Our cats are living longer and we are delighted that our cherished companions are sharing more time with us. However, sometimes we can take for granted the things which make us most comfortable in life – the ever-present and helping parent, the worn-in shoes that are like a second skin, the oft-quoted piece of furniture. Cats especially can live long and healthy lives and fit in so closely with our lifestyle that we almost forget they are there, or at least assume they will always be there. It is not until they become unwell or start asking for attention because they are feeling less secure that we suddenly realise that they have been with us for thirteen or fourteen years and sometimes a great deal longer. Cats are their own worst enemy when it comes to sympathy for ageing; they usually grow old very gracefully and seldom limp, sag or smell like older dogs tend to do! When they do become ill we sit down and wonder why we didn't pick up the signs earlier – when did they start drinking more? When did they start avoiding the stairs? When did they start to lose weight or their coat become dull?

This book is written around the questions, findings and comments of cat owners who completed a survey about old cats. These owners were overwhelmingly warm and appreciative of their old cats and treasured them greatly.

The Nine Life Cat aims to help owners of cats of all ages to keep an eye on their pets as the years go by; signs to look out for, behaviours to take note of, etc. which may just give a clue that something is amiss. Good health starts in kittenhood but there are lots of things we can do to keep our beloved cats as fit as possible throughout their lives and as comfortable as possible in their golden years. As well as physical problems, cats may also feel less secure as time goes on and may begin to call out at night or follow their owners around for reassurance. These and other changes in behaviour are discussed as well as the more common veterinary problems which older cats may suffer from.

The feelings which came from owners as they talked about their old cats were very deep. These cats live with us, usually getting on without fuss and when they eventually go, they leave a large hole in our lives. To know that we have done our best by them and that they have had a comfortable and happy life is a fitting and acceptable conclusion to many years of companionship.

What happens at the end is the culmination of all the previous years; it goes without saying that prevention is better than cure. What you feed and how you care for the kitten you have today may have a strong bearing on how well and fit your old cat stays in its twilight years. Make sure your cat enjoys his full nine lives.

1

Cat Years

Cats can live in good health for an amazingly long time considering their small size and comparing their longevity with that of dogs makes this even more incredible. Unlike cats, there is a huge variation in height, weight and shape of the dogs that make up the range of breeds we all know and love, with an equally wide range of average life spans – from around six or seven years for Irish Wolfhounds to about twelve for the more average-sized dogs. Mongrels often live to mid or late teens, while the oldest dog on record lived to a remarkable 27.

Cats are a more consistent species, however, and a well-cared-for cat will commonly live to fifteen, while some make it to eighteen or twenty, if not struck down by accident or disease. A few even more extraordinary felines pass the quarter-century mark. In fact, the cat is longer lived than almost all other domestic pets. The oldest feline recorded in the *Guinness Book of Records* was Puss, a tabby tom from Cullompton in Devon, who died the day after his thirty-sixth birthday in 1939. Perhaps the pure air, the warmer climate or the quality of the clotted cream had something to do with his longevity, because the oldest recorded female cat also lived in Devon. She died in 1957, aged 34. Unfortunately, we have no details of their lifestyle or youth-preserving secrets, but it is interesting to note that there are no more recent challengers – unless there is a puss out there somewhere lazily clocking up the years to put in a more up-to-date record.

KEEPING THE KITTEN IN YOUR CAT

We may not have a record-breaking old-aged cat living just at present, although there is a 31-year-old still going strong in the UK, but there is no doubt that increasing knowledge and technological know-how are enabling veterinary surgeons to help cats in general lead longer and healthier lives. We also know much more about the nutritional needs of our cats (a subject dealt with in detail in chapter 5). So, now, not only can we give them the best start in life, but we can also feed them according to their needs throughout life, both in health and sickness.

Changing attitudes, too, have enabled us all to love and enjoy our pets, lavishing them with attention and warmth and providing them with safe dens for refuge. Not so long ago, cats were merely rodent controllers and survived, as they can do so very well, by hunting, scavenging and partial feeding by cat lovers. The feral of today still lives on its wits, but no doubt it has a much shorter span of time on the earth than most of its pet counterparts – neutered and living in a colony that is being looked after by feeders it would be very lucky to live to ten years old.

The life expectancy of a solitary tom is said to be as low as two to three years because of his high-risk lifestyle. Roaming and fighting bring him closer to encounters with disease and cars. It is thought

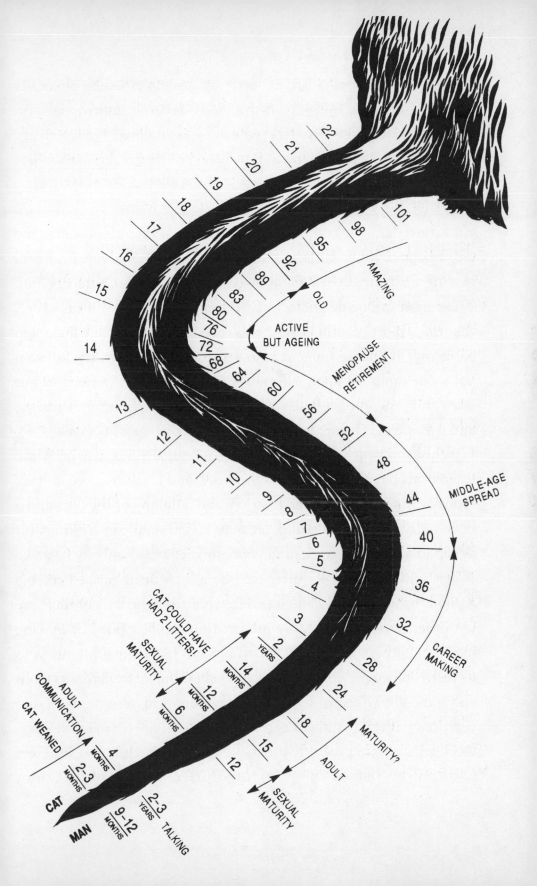

that the domestic cat's life expectancy has increased by about six years in the past thirty years because of better nutritional and veterinary care. So, where ten years old was accepted as a 'good' age for an aged feline, fourteen to sixteen is now nearer the mark.

AGELESS AGEING

Cats show dramatic body changes in their first year of life, emerging as sleek and lithe, athletic adults (well, most of them do!) and leaving far behind their bumblingly skittish, plump kitten bodies. Their most annoying characteristic from a human point of view is that these most beautiful of animals then show remarkably little sign of ageing. While we humans plan sensible diets, jog to try and slim away our tummies, apply all manner of lotions and potions to our skins and generally get it all wrong, the cat sleeps, hunts and washes, and it has barely a grey hair on its body by the age of twelve.

Whiskers, which have been dark throughout life, may go white (many cats have white whiskers anyway), and black coats go a shade browner; there may be some hair loss and a dulling of the coat and a little weight loss; but it is difficult to age a cat simply by looking at it asleep in a chair. Its grace of movement is equalled only by its grace of ageing. Looking closer there may be a little distinguished greying around the muzzle and sometimes elsewhere in the coat, but there are few other obvious signs. More information can be gained by looking in the mouth – an older cat, which has not had regular attention to its teeth and gums, will probably have a build-up of tartar on its teeth and some gum disease. Tooth loss is common in very old cats, and veterinary dental treatment can help maintain life for many years.

Older cats are probably a little more laid-back about life, less bothered by sudden noises or inquisitive dogs. They may not move with quite the same fluidity as they did in their prime. Changes may have been occurring gradually inside from as early as seven years old but, like the elegant glide of the swan over the lake, while paddling madly under the water beneath, the ageing of cats appears smooth and imperceptible. What owners have to do is look out for the small clues.

HOLDING BACK THE YEARS

It becomes much easier to understand how to manage our cats' lives and health and to understand their behaviour if we can associate their age with an equivalent of our own human years. Cats obviously mature much more rapidly than people, but from about three years old they seem to be ageless, suspended at the sensible, adult stage forever. Because we live so closely with them, their maturity, increasing wisdom and gentle slowing up are usually lost on us, and we may not realise that actually we have become guardians of very old and, by now, very treasured pets.

It is only when we look back that we acknowledge that the cat who used to be the pet of a single person, has coped with another person moving in, lived through at least four house moves, survived the poking fingers of several toddlers, been dressed up and pushed around in a pram by countless children, suitably disciplined the family puppy, snuggled up warm with the same dog in its old age, waved the children off to work or university and now fills an emotional gap in a much quieter household. It is then that we fully comprehend that puss has been around for a long time.

To children, the cat is a symbol of the warmth and permanence of the family unit and, for them, the cat has always been there – no wonder we miss our pets when they are gone. What is more, our cat has taken all the changes in its stride and would no doubt have a wealth of family stories to tell. It has been present, absorbing family life from its secret hiding places, ideal for catching snatches of conversation and family drama, listening to secret angers whispered by aggrieved children or absorbing tears of love or loss – perhaps it is just as well that cats can't talk.

A friend mourned the death of her eighteen-year-old cat for reasons beyond missing his larger-than-life personality – he had strong associations with a wonderful childhood and a rambling old house, and he was the last link with the family, which had split up a few years later. He represented the family bond and, even though the parting was many years earlier and all participants were happily settled again, the last living part of the memory was lost when he died.

CALCULATING A CAT'S AGE

The often recounted way of comparing a cat's or dog's age with that of a human being is to multiply its age by seven. Thus a one-year-old would be seven, a two-year-old fourteen, a twelve-year-old 96 and a twenty-year-old 140 and so on. However, this does not really equate very well with the life stages of the cat, and we now have a much better comparative method, which makes a great deal more sense. Here's how to calculate your cat's age in human terms: the first year of the cat's life can be taken as equivalent to fifteen human years; by the time it is two, the cat can be considered the equivalent of a 24-year-old person; thereafter each year can be taken as four human years. Thus a twelve-year-old is 64 (24 + [10 x 4]). If the cat is lucky enough to live past sixteen, the years after this can probably be taken to be the equivalent of about three human years.

When you start to look at a cat's life, all of this makes a great deal more sense. For example, in its first year the cat becomes weaned, learns to be independent of its mother, to hunt and live with a new family, and it is usually sexually mature by one year old (some as young as six months). Most humans, too, are physically able to reproduce by the age of fifteen. A two-year-old cat is quite an experienced creature and has just about fathomed out routines, and what it wants from those around it, as well as how to control them if they step out of line – some humans may have sorted this out by the age of 24!

A cat can be considered to be middle-aged by the time it is about eight years old and, in the same way as the ravages of age seem to affect some people more than others, the threshold from middle to old age is equally indefinite in cats – it can be anything from eight to sixteen. Just as some people are still able to run a marathon at 70 or continue with their hill-walking hobbies until they are 82, some cats will be happy to keep bringing in the mice until they are twenty, while others complain if they have to jump up on to the feeding bench at the age of ten. If you consider twelve as the age by which the cat should be drawing its pension, then the fifteen-year-old cat would be a credible 76, and the twenty-year-old almost as rare as a 92-year-old person. Those very uncommon cats, which live to over 30 – more than 124 years old – are, as yet, unexplainable and should perhaps have their names changed to Methuselah at a special ceremony.

A REPRODUCTIVE MARATHON

Although by using our new system we can sensibly compare the age of female sexual maturity in cats with that of humans and come out with a credible age – to within ten or fifteen years – the reproductive life of the cat is a great deal longer and has infinitely greater capacity than a man or woman's. A tabby cat called Dusty, who hailed from

Texas, produced her 420th kitten when she was eighteen years old in 1952. If she had three litters a year, she would have been pregnant 54 times with an average litter size of seven kittens. Bearing in mind that litter sizes drop after about 8 or 9 years old, she must have been extremely fertile in her younger years. Consider, too, that she would have been the equivalent of 86 during her final confinement!

The British record is held by another tabby – Tippy from Humberside – who produced her 343rd kitten when she was 21. Tish, a black-and-white geriatric mother produced her 100th and 101st kittens in 1958 aged 25 – it is too fantastic even to work out. Stories also tell of Smitty, a tortoiseshell, who had her first and only kitten aged 28 years old, after retiring from a lifetime of rat catching. It is certainly a long time to wait for this happy event, and at an age when most of us would be happy to be great- or even great-great-grandmothers and give the smiling baby a cuddle before handing it back to its mum when it begins to cry.

Healthy queens can usually produce kittens up to about twelve years old, and so obviously they do not go through the equivalent of the human female menopause. Perhaps this has something to do with the fact that female cats only ovulate after mating and do not have a regular ovulatory cycle the way humans do. As the queen ages beyond about eight years old, the litter size usually decreases, while after eleven or twelve years old many matings are unproductive. Most cat breeders have their queens spayed before this happens. Toms, like the males of most species, are potent for considerably longer, although the entire tom living an outdoor life has many hazards in his time, which will probably shorten his life considerably. However, if they can survive life's rigours, toms can usually mate successfully and sire offspring at up to fifteen or sixteen years old.

NORMAL BODY CHANGES WITH AGEING

We often put down an animal's frailties or illness to 'old age', and this is how we maybe writing off our pets without giving them the chance to prove otherwise, or the veterinary profession the opportunity to provide help or even a cure. There are, indeed, many predictable changes that occur naturally with passing years, but these do not necessarily cause illness. This is one of the areas with which researchers are still coming to grips – understanding the distinction between the ageing and the disease process. So what sort of changes go on in a cat's body as it gets older, and when do all these things begin to happen?

THE SEVEN-YEAR SWITCH

At about 7 years old, the cat's internal systems will start to slow down, and it can be said to be entering 'middle age' – the point in life when we humans start going to healthy-women or well-men clinics just to check that everything is ticking along all right. In the cat, ageing may not be noticeable from the outside, and, indeed, up to ten or twelve years old there may be very little overt change. However, it is important to be aware of some of the changes inside the body, in order to spot any problems or abnormalities that may arise. You should then point them out to your vet immediately.

As a cat gets older its metabolic rate slows down, hormone production is reduced, including those hormones that are critical to maintaining its normal body temperature. Its ability to regulate its own temperature diminishes – this happens regardless of the temperature outside its body, so obviously if it is a cold day it will be affected even more. Very cold weather could cause hypothermia in old animals just as it can in old people. This is why old cats are so good at finding the most cosy or hot spots in which to sleep away the hours.

Because the circulation is not as robust as it was, the cells of the skin may not receive as much oxygen as they once did – this combined with a less meticulous attitude or vigour of grooming and internal hormonal changes may mean that the cat's coat looks dull, and the hair may clump together giving it a spiky appearance. The sebaceous glands may not produce so much oil, therefore the coat is not so glossy. In extreme old age, there may be hair loss because hair follicles are less active and not replacing the hair as quickly as it is being lost. The skin is also less elastic and may be damaged more easily. Combine this with a slower repair system and a less efficient immune system, and the need to check old cats for bites or scratches and to keep an eye on them is paramount. Whereas a wound on a young cat will probably heal over in a day or two, in the older cat it may remain open and be more susceptible to infection. Likewise tumours are more likely to form in and under the skin.

Smell and taste are often dulled as ageing progresses – tastebud numbers decline, and the sense of smell is often the first sensory system to show the effects of age. This may cause a loss of appetite. Tartar may also build up on the teeth and push the gums back, allowing bacteria to enter the pockets of space around the base of the teeth and infect the gums. Less saliva is produced, which in turn means less protection for the teeth. In addition, changes occur in the eye as it ages, leading to thickening of the lens, and some cats may develop cataracts, causing sight impairment or blindness. Hearing may also become less acute as internal changes in the ear make it less sensitive, and wax may also accumulate, dulling those sounds that can get through.

The digestive system itself will become less efficient at absorbing all the animal needs from its diet, and the cat may not be able to cope with large meals but wish to eat little and often, enabling its body to take its time and get the most from the small portions. In general, the old cat loses muscle volume and tone, and it is less flexible, moving more slowly and with diminished agility. Although dogs suffer more commonly from arthritis, cats, too, may experience pain when they move and may begin to lose their feline fluidity and stiffen up. Because less blood reaches the muscles, they are not able to maintain long periods of work. Thus the cat is tired after short bursts of running or climbing. Of course, these changes are very gradual and may not become apparent until the cat is twelve or thirteen years old.

As in mankind, old age brings with it the likelihood of heart and lung disease and, although these are not such a problem in the feline world, the normal ageing process does render the systems less efficient and more susceptible to problems. The urinary system, too, gradually declines as the years pass, and the kidneys are less able to deal with the load put upon them. With age kidneys lose some of their ability to concentrate urine, and so the volume of urine will be larger and more dilute, and the cat may need to urinate more frequently. The kidneys may not be able to filter the blood as well as they used to, and toxins can build up in the body. The bladder also becomes less elastic and may not empty totally each time the cat urinates – this may lead to increased susceptibility to infection, so keep an eye on the cat in case it is suffering from cystitis.

Loss of muscle tone may also mean that accidents can occur when the cat has not managed to reach the garden or the litter tray in time. One of the first signs of senility is loss of house training.

Finally, changes occur to the nervous system, which make old cats slower to react or learn. If senility does become a problem, the cat may become irritable if disturbed and have difficulty with orientation – some have been known to wander and get lost.

PREVENTION IS BETTER THAN CURE

None of us really wants to face the changes that occur in our bodies simply because of the passage of time and, listed like this, they may seem depressing. However, while ageing comes to us all, how we look after ourselves and, in this case, our cats may mean that its effects can be delayed or complications prevented as we grow old gracefully. Cats don't appear to worry about getting older – nor do they need to. They may feel frustrated because they can not do everything they want or climb up to where they want to be – but then they have us human carers to ensure that this does not cause too much of a problem for them. Most cats, at least in the Western world, have a human safety net to cushion them in their declining years and faculties.

Old age should be regarded not as a disease, but rather as a state in which the cat is not so good at surviving stress and less able to adjust to change. If we take our system of calculating a cat's age, we might change our minds about the longevity chances of a ten-year-old pet. How would you feel if your doctor wrote you off at 56 because you were 'old'? To match our life expectancy of about 80 years, the cat needs to survive to sixteen. The ability of our pets to do so lies, to a great extent, with their owners – with how they treat them in their early years and how much care and attention they give them later. Prevention is definitely better than cure and, although ageing cannot be suspended, many of the complications of disease associated with the ageing process can be lessened if caught early enough. So just how can you try to keep the kitten in your cat and make sure he gets his full nine lives?

2

Nine Lives?

What is the secret of a cat's longevity? Before we look at its lifestyle and secrets, there are more obvious factors that must be taken into account, which explain why some cats live a full, long and healthy life, while others have but a brief time with us.

An interesting set of statistics from the United States presented at a conference on geriatric pets highlighted one of the most dangerous times of a cat's life. Researchers investigated the average survival age of a group of cats – calculating the average from the research group – and they came up with a figure of eight years. Now any cat owner will tell you that their cat is merely at its peak at eight years old – after all, this is equivalent to people only living to about 50.

Something was definitely amiss. The researchers then followed the lives of a group of cats from the age of one year onwards. Their average age at death was found to be twelve, an average we would accept as about right, at between 60 and 70 years old. So why the large discrepancy? Removing from the equation those cats that died in their first year gave the average age with which we are familiar and which we accept from experience. The fact is that the first year of a cat's life is the most hazardous – it must learn to survive away from its mother, become sexually mature and cope with all the dangers of life – not least of which is the motor-car.

FELINE ENEMY NO. 1

It is thought that between 30 to 40 per cent of cats that die each year are killed on the road. No doubt almost as many cat owners will have experienced the death of their cat in a road accident as will have seen them die of old age. Although those cats killed on the road are not by any means always aged under one year old, most older cats have figured out how and when to cross the road – or not to cross at all. We all know how children dart across the road to see a friend or simply wander across without looking because they have something else on their minds. In fact, human psychologists believe that a child is not safe to cross the road alone until the age of seven. So it is with cats. Young cats can dash across the street with territorial combatants in pursuit or rush to greet the cat over the road or merely panic at the sight of the traffic, and drivers don't stand a chance of stopping in time.

Whoever gave the cat the benefit of nine lives probably lived before the age of traffic. Although most dangerous encounters with people or other animals can be escaped with only one of nine lives lost, the car has no respect of this lore and will take all nine at once. We have all had narrow escapes and learned from our experiences, and young cats equally discover through trial and error – what to jump on or over, which dogs to give a wide berth and which animals to hunt. The trouble is that making a mistake with a car is usually fatal, and trial and error learning can be very risky here. Many people who live near roads keep their animals indoors permanently because of previous heartbreaking losses. However, those who get another cat can usually breathe a sigh of relief if it is still with them after the first few months of exploration, and after one year they feel confident it may have sussed out the road-crossing system successfully. Many people who live near busy roads or who just wish to keep their cats ultra-safe, fence in their gardens or build a large run where the cat can go out in the fresh air but still be secure. The Feline Advisory Bureau (see contact details at the back) has information on how to do this.

Many young cats also have other sorts of accidents or get stuck in such dangerous places as drains or the washing machine. They tend to jump on to the hot oven-hob or chew poisonous plants because they are exploring and inexperienced at recognising all the dangers around - after all, this is the way they learn.

PREVENTATIVE CARE – START YOUNG

It may sound strange, but it is important that caring for the health of your elderly cat should start when it is a few weeks old. Just as we now realise that diet, preventative healthcare, such as vaccinations, and lifestyle during childhood can have a profound effect upon health in later life, we also know that there is a lot that can be done in early life to improve the long-term health of animals. Of course, we have all heard of a healthy 90-year-old man, who smoked like a chimney and drank like a fish all his life (and usually has no intention of stopping now!), and similarly we come across battered old tom-cats that have never been near a vet in their lives. Life's a lottery, and by taking care to give your cat the best possible start you will increase the odds of that cat living to a healthy old age.

WHAT ABOUT BREEDING?

Among dogs, breed can have a marked influence upon life expectancy – a small dog such as a Jack Russell Terrier could well hope to live to fourteen or sixteen, whereas a giant breed such as a Great Dane really does begin to feel its age by the time it reaches around eight. Because man has bred dogs in such a wide range of shapes and sizes, we see marked hybrid vigour. This means that crossbreeds and mongrels have a more robust constitution and generally better health. With their greater mix of genes, they are less likely to carry hereditary diseases and more likely to have a body shape closer to that of a 'normal' dog.

Cat breeds have avoided the vast excesses of dog breeding, and by and large most pedigree cats are quite similar in size and overall shape to their moggie relatives. This is partly because, although both cats and dogs have had a long history of domestication, it is only in this century that the cat has been selectively bred to produce different body forms and coat types. Dogs, on the other hand, have been selectively bred to perform different working functions for thousands of years. It could also be argued that the strict rules of the Governing Council of the Cat Fancy (the organisation that governs cat breeding and showing) have also helped to discourage irresponsible breeding, refusing to recognise new breeds that have been bred in a way that affects their health. Serious hereditary diseases do occur and are more common in pedigree cats, but they are quite uncommon.

Although accurate figures on the life expectancy of different breeds of cats do not exist, pedigree cats do not seem to have a very different life expectancy from non-pedigree cats, and Breeds such as the Siamese and Burmese seem to be particularly long-lived. Among the pedigrees, the Siamese are said to be the longest lived, with a life expectancy of about fifteen years. Whether this is because they are one of the slimmer breeds and not so prone to obesity, it is hard to say, but anyone sharing their lives with a Siamese for over fifteen years usually has a real character on their hands by then. Siamese are not slow to let their feelings be known and usually manage to get their 'owners' to give in to their demands with slave-like devotion – and they don't get any less demanding with age (*see* chapter 6).

VACCINATIONS FOR LIFE

Kittens can normally start their vaccination course at nine weeks of age, and the benefits of early vaccination followed by regular booster injections will serve them well throughout their life. Most of the diseases against which we vaccinate cats are caused by viruses and, once they gain entry into the body, many can remain there for many years or even for life.

FELINE PANLEUCOPAENIA

The oldest feline vaccine is against feline panleucopaenia, also known as feline infectious enteritis, a very severe form of viral gastroenteritis that mainly affects younger cats and can rapidly result in death. This virus is very much a 'kill or cure' agent, and in years gone past claimed the lives of many cats.

CAT FLU

This is not the case with the cat-flu viruses, rather incorrectly named because they are not caused by influenza viruses, as in humans, and the disease they cause is often much more severe than a bout of human flu. You can therefore also rest assured that you cannot transmit human flu to your cat, or vice versa. There are two main viruses that cause cat flu: feline calicivirus and feline herpesvirus. The latter is particularly persistent and, once infected, a cat will often remain a carrier throughout its life, developing signs of a runny nose and runny eyes whenever it is stressed and the virus overcomes the body's defences.

Apart from carrying the virus, some cats that are severely infected with cat flu are left with such severe damage to the lining of the passages in the nose that they develop a chronic rhinitis – often referred to as 'snufflers' because of the congestive snuffly noises the cats make when breathing. Other agents, such as the the bacteria *Chlamydophila felis* and *Bordetella brondriseptica*, also cause milder forms of what is loosely described as cat flu. Chlamydophila infection produces mainly runny eyes, and a vaccine is now available which is used primarily in colonies of cats where such infections have proved a problem.

Bordetella bronchiseptica is now known to be a significant cause of upper-respiratory signs in cats. It also causes kennel cough in dogs, and there is evidence to suggest it may be transmissible from one species to the other. An intranasal (drops in the nose) vaccine against this organism has recently become available in the UK and, although it is not likely to become part of the mainstream vaccination programme for cats, it will be useful in a cattery situation where bordetella is known to be a problem.

FELINE LEUKAEMIA

We are very fortunate that a vaccine has been developed against feline leukaemia virus (FeLV), since this agent is one of the most serious of diseases that can affect the cat. About 1 per cent of cats are infected. Surveys of sick cats have found that up to 18 per cent had the virus in their blood. The virus can cause four main groups of signs:

- A potentially fatal and severe anaemia
- Infertility
- Damage to the immune system that can cause the cat to contract a wide range of secondary infections
- Tumour development, particularly lymphosarcoma, a cancer of the white blood cells

Due to the effects of feline leukaemia virus infection, cancers of the white blood cells are by far the most common tumour affecting the cat. Many older cats develop this form of cancer late in life, and the virus is often no longer detectable in the blood but has incorporated itself into the genetic matter within the body cells themselves. It is possible for the virus to be passed on to future generations before birth, nevertheless it is hoped that widespread vaccination will dramatically reduce the incidence of these types of disease in the cat.

FELINE IMMUNODEFICIENCY

Unfortunately, despite being the most simple form of life, viruses have proved extremely difficult to conquer because they can mutate and develop new forms very rapidly. Such a virus, called feline immunodeficiency virus, or FIV, is similar to the agent that causes AIDS in humans. The virus damages the immune system and, just like human AIDS can manifest itself in many different ways. The cat can become infected with secondary agents that would not normally trouble it but are able to take advantage of its lowered resistance.

It is estimated that 3 to 6 per cent of healthy cats are infected and in surveys of sick cats this figure can increase to over 12 per cent. A vaccine against the disease has recently been introduced in the United States, but there is limited data as to its efficacy at this point. In the UK, where the onus to prove the effectiveness of a medicinal product before a licence is granted is more stringent, it seems that it will be some time before one is available. However, cats that are carrying the virus may be able to live relatively normal lives for several years. There has been no evidence to show that either the feline immunodeficiency or leukaemia viruses are transmissible to humans.

REGULAR BOOSTERS

It can be seen that vaccinations from an early age can have a very marked bearing upon the health of a cat in later life as, once many of these viruses get into the body, the cat may not be able to get rid of them and vaccination in later life would then have no effect (although vaccination is better late than never – just in case). Your cat should receive an annual health check combined with a review of its vaccination status. The decision as to whether all the booster vaccinations should be given every year will depend very much upon your cat's individual circumstances.

WE ARE WHAT WE EAT

We are what we eat – this well-known adage applies just as much to cats as to us humans. Specific diets for elderly cats will be dealt with later, but it follows that a well-balanced diet early on in life will set the foundations for a healthy future. We are fortunate that the large pet-food manufacturers expend a great deal of resources in developing diets that are ideal for our pet cats.

Canned cat foods are big business, an annual UK turnover of over £530 million making them among the biggest-selling branded grocery products on the supermarket shelves and outselling canned dog foods by over £200 million a year. It seems, however, that we still want to spend even more on pampering our cats, and the trend is towards smaller, foil-wrapped 'gourmet' cat foods with such mouthwatering ingredients as salmon, trout and shrimp.

Many cats also seem to enjoy eating dry cat foods, which have basically the same contents as the canned product but a much lower moisture content of about 12 per cent (canned cat foods contain about 75 per cent water).

MEAT TO LIVE

Whether you choose to pamper your cat or feed it one of the budget brands of cat food, you can rest assured that all the complete foods provided by the major manufacturers will provide a balanced diet. Cats have very particular nutritional requirements and, for example, should not be fed on dog food, which could cause deficiencies to develop in the long run. Whatever your own beliefs, it is also dangerous to feed a cat on a vegetarian diet. Cats are obligate carnivores and, while omnivorous animals, such as man and even the dog, are able to obtain all the nutrients they need from a vegetarian diet, cats have lost this ability and will incur severe deficiencies leading to poor coat quality, heart disease and even blindness. Eat soya and beans yourself by all means, but it's meat for the cat.

Of course, this does not mean that it is not possible to feed a cat a perfectly satisfactory diet of fresh foods, simply that you have to be more careful to ensure that the overall intake is properly balanced. Many owners feed canned foods on a regular basis and fresh as an occasional treat. Do ensure that you provide a wide variety of different foods and that you do not allow your cat to get faddy and hooked on one particular fresh food. For example, too much liver in the diet can cause an overdose of vitamin A, which might cause an inflammation of the bones in the neck and forelimbs, and too much raw fish can cause nervous disorders due to a deficiency of thiamine, one of the B vitamins.

LET'S TALK ABOUT SEX

By and large, it is perhaps a good thing that there is little choice about neutering pet cats, as it saves them from many disease problems in later life that are common in entire cats – and this is particularly true in the cases of females.

QUEENS

Whereas it is relatively easy to keep an unspayed bitch under control for her season a couple of times each year, an unspayed queen will come into season and 'call' for a few days about every three weeks during her breeding season in late winter and early summer. This is not only tiring for the cat but can also be extremely exhausting for its owner, as 'calling' is a very appropriate name for the yowling that emanates from many a queen doing what comes naturally in her attempts to attract a mate. Calling ceases rapidly after mating, but the entire female cat, when allowed to fulfil her breeding potential, very rapidly becomes a kitten factory, churning out two or even three litters a year. Although the frequency of the seasons and fertility decrease with age, queens can give birth at quite an advanced age. However, as almost all pet female cats will have been neutered well before old age, problems related to the production of female hormones, such as womb infections, breast cancer and tumours of the reproductive tract, are rare.

TOMS

There are different, if equally compelling, reasons for neutering a male cat. An entire tom-cat will develop behaviour patterns that make it quite unsuitable as a pet. He will spend days at a time wandering around a large patch of territory, which he will defend fiercely from other male cats, often returning from his war campaigns with a collection of battle scars. Any cat may sometimes mark its territory by spraying urine in certain places, but this is much more common in tom-cats, who also come equipped with particularly pungent-smelling urine. The owner of an entire tom will soon find out who his really loyal friends are. Although the health benefits from castrating a male cat are less obvious than with a female, the years of fighting do usually take their toll, especially as the tom-cat becomes older, more frail and less likely to win his battles. Additionally the close contact of a cat fight also provides an excellent opportunity for the transmission of disease such as feline immunodeficiency virus which is spread solely by biting, or simply from bite wounds becoming infected.

FAT AND THE NEUTERED CAT

The only disadvantage of neutering is the tendency for cats to become less active and put on weight, although even neutered cats are quite good at regulating their food intake and certainly more so than dogs. Cats do not commonly suffer from heart disease or arthritis – two serious problems that could be aggravated by obesity – but they are prone to diabetes, which is aggravated if the cat is overweight. It is also rather difficult to modify the food intake of the average cat – it knows exactly how to make its owner's life pure hell if it does not get what it wants to eat and, if all else fails, it will raid the neighbours' dustbins. Some people suggest that as many as 50 per cent of cats are now overweight.

However, new highly palatable yet reduced-calorie cat foods are now available, and changing your cat on to this type of food or adding a little extra roughage into the diet in the form of wheat bran at the first sign of excessive weight gain will help to control the problem. Avoid feeding large amounts of the ordinary dry cat foods to a plump puss as they are very dense in calories and do encourage weight gain. It is certainly very much easier to make relatively fine adjustments to the diet and prevent your cat from getting fat than to try to get those extra inches off once they are there.

WORMING/FLEA CONTROL

All cats will have worms at some times in their lives. The permanently indoor cat obviously stands less risk of ingesting worm eggs, but they may have been passed on to them via the queen's milk when very young. A cat that regularly goes outdoors, hunts and eats its prey obviously stands a much greater risk of becoming host to either roundworms or tapeworms. Flea larvae may ingest tapeworm eggs and infect cats when they bite, so flea control is also a factor in worm control. Although neither worm will cause great harm to adult cats (small kittens are often more severely affected by roundworms), they may make them feel slightly under the weather and are best treated regularly to keep the cat at peak fitness. Treatment is simple and effective with drugs available from our vets, and because we now live so closely with our pets it is best for the health and hygiene of the whole family if there is no risk of worms passing from cats to people.

Fortunately for owners who find dosing their cat with tablets challenging, there are now spot-on veterinary products that can be used to treat fleas, roundworms and tapeworms (but not a single one that covers all three) by spotting a few drops of liquid from a sachet on to the back of the neck.

TOOTHCARE

It may seem a little odd to mention toothcare as one of the main factors affecting longevity in the cat; however, if it cannot eat, is in constant pain or its body is affected by a mouth infection, then your cat's health will be severely hampered. Many tooth and gum problems can be prevented or treated by the vet – more of this in chapters 3 and 4.

LUXURY LIFESTYLES

'It is thought that a properly fed, confined cat at sixteen years old is at the same stage of ageing, physiologically, as an intact, free-roaming eight-year-old cat.' This is a quote from a veterinary textbook, and it provides an excellent example of how our 'domestication' of the cat can affect its longevity. By keeping cats indoors, we remove the dangers of car accidents, malice from cat haters, danger from dogs and other cats, the perils of poisoning (either deliberate or by eating poisoned prey) and the risk of infection with disease from other cats.

However, we must also take into account quality of life and the individual personalities of our cats. Some will be quite happy to laze away their days indoors and have no yearning for excitement and the thrill of the hunt or need for variety. Others are more active and require stimulation if they are not to become somewhat neurotic with our imprisonment – they do not know we are keeping them in for their own safety. Most cat owners, if at all possible, will let their cats live out that other side of their character – the outdoor hunter and territory maker – and it would not be fair to keep cats in just because we think they may live longer.

SPEED OF TREATMENT – OWNER CARE

Although some lucky cats may go through life without the need for any special or emergency veterinary care, most will need help at some point, especially as the years march on. Just how well they recover or cope with problems can be entirely dependent on the speed with which their owners first notice the problem and then act to do something about it. This fast action is important throughout the cat's life but never more so than in old age. It is then that problems begin to occur in multiples – the younger pet probably had one thing wrong with it at a time, while the older animal may have several problems, which may also interact with each other, complicating the illness further. Just as human doctors now specialise in medical care for the elderly, veterinary surgeons are realising the importance of carefully examining each old cat for its own unique set of problems. They must examine all the body's systems, not just the obvious and presenting complaint. What they must also do is to separate the disease problem from the natural ageing process.

POWERS OF POSITIVE THINKING

Many owners fear that if they take an unfit or ailing older cat to their vet that he or she will advise euthanasia because of 'age', not because of the problem. This is now certainly not the case, and recent advances in veterinary care mean that many previously fatal diseases can be tackled successfully. Even if the problem is not curable, much can be done to slow down the progression of the disease and give the cat many more pain-free and comfortable weeks, or even years, to enjoy with its family.

Having a positive attitude and acting quickly could save your cat's life. Early treatment is much more likely to be successful. You are the greatest single factor determining how long the animal will live. Just what to look out for, both medically and behaviourally, is outlined in the following chapters. Never underestimate your cat's will to live and ability to cope. Veterinary surgeons are also learning more and more about old cats – be guided by their advice. One open-minded cat owner wrote a wonderful letter to the *Feline Advisory Bureau Journal* to encourage others on just such a matter. It will bring a tear to the eye of any cat owner, young or old.

Tuffy is a 13-year-old neutered male Shorthair. From the day he was old enough to hiss ferociously when he was picked up, he made it plain that he was going to be his own cat, a free independent spirit. He would come and go as he wished, he would not be confined to being a mother's boy, a purring lap-cat. Even though his mother was, and still is, loving and gentle, he has always been a prime example of the influence of heredity over environment. It was all the more tragic then when he developed cataracts in both eyes during last winter.

By spring the vet confirmed that, if not totally blind already, he soon would be. However, I was told, 'Give him a chance, you will be surprised how well he adapts,' and adapt he did – there was nothing wrong with his memory, he knew the best ways to get over the garden fence, where his tray was kept and how to get round the house. He changed his routine so that he only went out at night when he could hear what was happening and there was no traffic in the cul-de-sac where he played. He still gave me a few sleepless nights while I worried in case he got lost, in case he fell from a fence or in case he developed glaucoma in his unseeing eyes.

Then fate gave him another sharp kick in the head. I came home from work to find him half-sitting, half-lying, weaving his head snakily from side to side, obviously distressed. My first reaction was that his eyes had developed more trouble, but the vet said no, this time he had had a stroke, a bad one. His head seemed too heavy for his neck, he could barely walk and was staggering badly from side to side. Then again I heard the magic words, 'Give him a chance, you will be surprised how well he adapts.'

This time I didn't really believe it, surely the kindest thing would be to put this poor confused animal out of the misery he must surely be feeling. However, I decided not to overrule the vet's expert opinion and demand the 'final injection' – I took her advice and gave him a chance. I was told that his sense of balance was affected and his loss of sight would make this worse since he could not see the horizon. He would probably always carry his head tilted, but he would adapt.

Adapt he has – his ungainly lurch from side to side has calmed down to a gentle weaving motion, unless he is under stress for some reason, then he goes round very fast in tight circles, obviously under the impression he is travelling in a straight line. He cannot raise his head to look upwards, he no longer jumps over the garden fence, but he still spends a lot of his time outdoors circling round at the bottom of the garden. He no longer leaps up on to the bed or chair, instead he climbs up slowly, paw over paw. When he wants to get down, he lowers his head, shoulders and forearms as far as he can and then falls off, landing inelegantly but safety on the ground below.

He eats well, uses his tray without difficulty and stands no nonsense from anyone, cat or dog. He is still very strong, has lightning-fast reflexes and a ferocious right hook, which lands somewhere on target if anyone else gets stroppy. Also, as a result of all this trauma, he has become a little more trusting. I am allowed liberties he never permitted before – the occasional tickle behind the ear, a quick smoothing of ruffled fur, even the feeding of an especially tasty morsel by hand.

So, when the vet tells you, 'Give it a chance, you will be surprised how well they can adapt' – believe it, it's true!

Angela Slaid

INSURE FOR PEACE OF MIND

A sudden accident or illness can present an owner with an unexpected bill for veterinary fees. There is much that can be done with modern veterinary care to treat even the most severe problem, but a course of treatment could run to several hundred pounds.

Many cat owners are not aware that for around £2.00 a week they can take out pet insurance to cover veterinary costs – the owner only has to pay an initial excess of around £50 for any particular course of treatment, and the rest can be claimed back from the insurance company up to the policy limit, usually around several thousand pounds. Of course, preventative care such as vaccinations are not covered, but there are often other useful benefits included, such as payment for advertising and offering a reward for a lost cat, holiday cancellation costs if your cat needs emergency surgery before you go away on holiday, and boarding cattery fees if you have to go into hospital. Many of the cheaper policies will only cover a particular condition for a maximum of a year, whereas others will insure your cat for life. Compare the small print carefully and decide which one is best suited to your needs.

Most companies will only insure a cat if it is under 10 years of age when the policy is initially taken out, but then they will undertake to continue that cover for the rest of its life. Many cat owners have found pet insurance to be extremely worthwhile – all too many have only thought about taking out a policy once disaster has struck.

3

Staying In The Pink

Cats are generally quite maintenance-free, so if you are lucky you may not have to make too many visits to a vet while your cat is young, except for vaccinations and parasite control and perhaps the inevitable consequence of the occasional cat fight. As your cat gets older, however, problems become more common, and it is to your advantage to build up a good working relationship with a veterinary surgeon so that the vet gets to know your cat, and you get to know your vet.

FIRST, FIND A VET

So how should you go about finding a good practice? Many people simply use the vet that is closest to them, and there is certainly something to be said in favour of choosing a vet who is close to hand when needed, particularly if your cat is a bad traveller. The surgeries in your area will be listed in British Telecom's Yellow Pages and the Thomson Directory under 'Veterinary Surgeons and Practitioners'. The internet can be a very useful resource for finding a practice, as many have websites outlining their staff and facilities. You can access many of these via Yell.com, or using the search facility run by the Royal College of Veterinary Surgeons at www.findavet.org.uk.

But, there are other considerations, and first and foremost you will need to find someone who seems to care about your cat and who inspires your confidence. The facilities that are available for treatment are also important – the waiting-room should be clean and tidy, the staff friendly and well-trained, and the surgery should have modern equipment such as X-rays, gaseous anaesthesia and hospitalisation facilities. The Royal College of Veterinary Surgeons publishes a directory of veterinary practices, and those conforming to the recommended standards laid down by the British Small Animal Veterinary Association are marked accordingly – the directory should be available for inspection at any public library or on the web.

The British Veterinary Hospital Association lays down even more stringent regulations regarding the premises, equipment and nursing care available, and only practices conforming to these guidelines are allowed to describe themselves as 'Veterinary Hospitals'. All practices are ethically obliged to offer a 24-hour emergency service to their clients, although in some cases this may involve a rota with other neighbouring practices or with a central emergency clinic in the area.

SPECIALISTS

Recommendation from a reliable friend is an excellent means of selecting a practice, although at the end of the day there is no substitute for going along and trying one out. Once you have found a practice that suits you, do not chop and change. If you are not happy with the results of a particular course of treatment, discuss it with the veterinary surgeon caring for your cat.

If you still cannot see the way forward, ask your vet to arrange for a referral to a specialist for that particular type of problem. This is far preferable to just turning up at another veterinary surgery in the area and expecting another vet to take over the case. Veterinary surgeons are not ethically permitted to do this without first obtaining the permission of the vet who has already been treating the patient. More importantly, too, for the sake of the animal, it is also vital to have full details of all diagnostic tests and treatments that have been carried out already.

GETTING THERE

Cats should always be taken to a vet in a secure cat carrier, preferably made out of plastic or plastic-coated wire mesh so that it can easily be cleaned. Borrowing a basket is not a good idea, as there is always some risk of transmitting disease on the carrier itself, and you may need one quickly in an emergency. The same warning applies to the good Samaritans who lend out their carriers. Cardboard cat carriers are best avoided as a nervous cat will often urinate in the box. As well as being very messy, cardboard has a habit of disintegrating when it is soaked in urine, and the cat may well drop out of the bottom of the box during the journey.

MOTS FOR CATS?

Prevention is always better than cure. This cannot be said often enough. Booster vaccinations should be kept up throughout the life of a cat, not only to maintain protection against disease but also to allow the veterinary surgeon an opportunity to give the cat a health examination.

SENIOR PET PROGRAMMES

Many vets are now taking the role of prevention further by offering clients the chance to arrange for their cat to have a regular health screen in order to try and pick up disease problems early – often before the owner is really aware that a problem exists. A typical 'Senior Pet Programme' would include the following items:

- Thorough physical examination
- Discussion of diet and lifestyle
- Blood test
- Urine examination
- Blood pressure monitoring
- Further tests, such as X-rays and ultrasound, if necessary

There is no reason why this sort of in-depth health screening should not be carried out at any age, but most vets would recommend that it is carried out on at least an annual basis from around the age of eight. Cats are extremely good at masking signs of any problems until they become quite advanced, but it is rare not to turn up at least one minor problem in a cat of that age, such as early dental disease or the first signs of kidney problems.

In some cases, potentially very serious problems can be diagnosed and treated much more effectively than if the owner had waited until the cat showed obvious signs of illness. For example, Dusty was a seemingly fit ten-year-old cat, which was brought for a health screen and found to have a liver tumour developing. It was possible surgically to cut out the tumour before it spread elsewhere within the body or became too large to remove, and Dusty went on to live for three more contented years before he died of a completely unrelated cause.

ADVANCED ANAESTHETICS

Anaesthetics are now much safer than they were twenty or thirty years ago, and it is now not unusual to carry out operations on even the most elderly of cats. While veterinary surgeons will not wish to carry out procedures under anaesthetic that are not entirely necessary for an older cat, age itself is no longer a contraindication for anaesthesia. If a problem is causing pain or discomfort or is likely significantly to shorten the lifespan of the cat if left untreated, then an operation may well be the best course of action. If your cat is suffering from a particular condition that may increase the anaesthetic risks, such as heart disease, the veterinary surgeon may well try to treat the problem medically beforehand. Each case has to be decided on its individual merit, and you should be guided by your veterinary surgeon on the decision of whether or not to operate.

HEALTH CHECKS TO MAKE AT HOME

Check over your cat regularly. It is amazing how many owners accept their animals as part of the furnishings and never really physically examine them. If you own a long-haired cat, you will probably have been in the habit of grooming it regularly throughout its life, and this is an ideal opportunity to check that all is well. Even short-haired cats may need grooming as they become elderly (*see* chapters 4 and 8).

It only takes a minute or two to give your cat a once-over, paying attention to the following list.

PHYSICAL CHECKPOINTS

Ears Any abnormal discharge may indicate infection or ear-mite infestation.

Eyes Look for signs of soreness or abnormal discharge. A slight watery discharge maybe normal, especially in some of the flat-nosed breeds, but there should not be a thick discharge. Some darkening of the iris (the coloured part of the eye around the pupil) is quite normal in some older cats.

Nose Again look for any abnormal discharges. If the cat has a pink, unpigmented nose, then a change in colour, such as pallor (*see* anaemia in chapter 4), may be noticeable.

Inside the mouth Check for any ulcers or soreness in the throat or on the tongue, or soreness of the gums, which may be caused by an accumulation of calculus (tartar) on the teeth – a brown discolouration of the teeth caused by a light accumulation of tartar may not be of any significance if it is not yet affecting the gums. Bad breath (halitosis) can be an indication of either a dental problem or of some more generalised disease such as kidney failure and should be reported to your vet.

Coat Check for any sores, scabs, loss of hair, scurfiness or poor coat quality. You may be able to see signs of fleas – very often you will not spot the fleas themselves, but the reddish-brown flea dirt that they leave behind (it is actually dried blood and will form a reddish-brown halo if put on to a piece of damp cotton wool). Fleas need to be tackled both on the cat and in the house.

Body Feel the body for any unusual lumps or bumps.

Paws Check the nails in case they have become overgrown (*see* overgrown nails, chapter 4).

Under the tail Look under the tail for any soiling of the anus, which might indicate that the cat is suffering from loose stools, and any signs of internal parasites such as tapeworm (the small rice-like segments can often be seen adhering to the hair under the tail).

Breathing Watch the normal breathing pattern of your cat. Respiratory problems are quite common in elderly cats, and the first sign could be laboured breathing even when the cat is relaxed and at rest. With more severe chest problems, the whole pattern of respiration may change, with the cat using its abdominal muscles to try and push air in and out of its chest.

Other than learning to spot actual physical abnormalities, you should also watch out for any changes in your cat's behaviour pattern. Most owners are very attuned to the normal routine of their own cat and get the feeling that something is not quite right before there are any obvious signs of illness. Behavioural changes that could be of particular significance are listed here.

BEHAVIOURAL CHECKPOINTS

Urinating in abnormal places A common place to choose is down the plughole of the bath (*see* cystitis, chapter 4).

An increased thirst Cats are very good at conserving body fluid, and some owners hardly ever see their cat drinking at all. However, increased thirst is a sign that can be an important indicator of several common diseases in the elderly cat. It is very difficult to monitor the fluid intake of cats that go outdoors, but you may well notice them going to the water bowl more frequently. You may also notice your cat suddenly starting to drink from a dripping tap or out of puddles.

Desire to go outdoors more frequently This could indicate that the cat is suffering from diarrhoea or cystitis (*see* chapter 4: cystitis; digestive upsets).

Change in eating patterns Any change in eating or a loss of appetite for more than a day or two can signal illness. Some cats are finicky eaters anyway and often skip meals, whereas some owners can set their watches by their cats' demanding food. It is the change in the pattern that is normal for your cat, which is important. You may also be able to detect that your cat has a sore mouth by the way that it eats the food once picked out of the bowl.

CHECKPOINT EARLY

If you are in any way concerned about the health of your cat, get veterinary advice. Many owners are concerned that they are 'troubling the vet unnecessarily', or that a serious problem might be identified, and the cat then be put to sleep. Remember that the vet is there to help you and should be only too happy to check a problem early on and hopefully to put your mind at rest. Remember also that the earlier any problem is identified, the more chance there is of it being easily corrected. There is a tremendous amount that can be done with modern veterinary medicine to cure or control many problems, which were until recently considered untreatable.

COLLECTING A SAMPLE

A urine sample can be very useful for the diagnosis of many problems in elderly cats, particularly those that cause the cat to drink more than normal. If your cat already uses a litter tray, then it is not usually too difficult to get it to use a well-cleaned tray that contains gravel (as used in fishtanks) or special non-absorbent litter from which the urine can be poured into a collecting bottle.

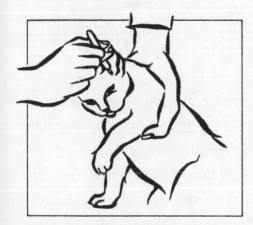 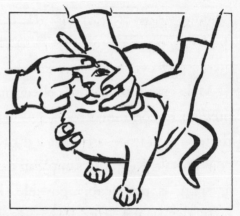

ADMINISTERING EAR DROPS

Any dirt and wax should be gently cleaned from the ear. Hold the ear flap and use a cotton-tipped stick, but do not insert it deeper than the depth of cotton tip. Than, keeping hold of the ear flap firmly, allow the drops to drip into the ear canal – the cat may resent it less if you warm the bottle of drops in your hands first.

Hold on to the ear flap long enough to allow the drops to run down deep into the ear. Clean away any excess ointment.

ADMINISTERING EYE DROPS

Hold the head of the cat as if administering a tablet, but do not bend it backwards. Approach with the bottle or tube from above, and either allow a drop to fall on to the surface of the eye, or pull the lower eyelid downward and put a small amount of ointment between the lower eyelid and the eye.

Do not touch the surface of the eye with the bottle or tube, and do not allow the end of the bottle or tube to become contaminated.

What is the matter with my cat?

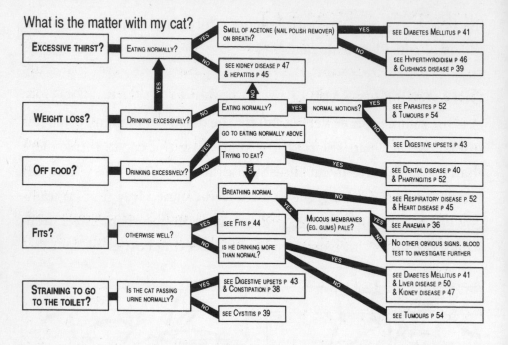

Make sure that the collecting bottle is also clean and, if it previously contained food, pay particular attention to ensure that there are no traces of sugar left or a false diagnosis of sugar diabetes could result. Keep the sample in a cool place and get it to the surgery as soon as practicably possible. If you have to collect a sample regularly, special litter trays with channels to collect urine and non-absorbent cat litter are available.

If your cat does not normally use a litter tray, you will have to confine it in an enclosed space with a litter tray until it has to resort to using the tray.

Vets often measure the rectal temperature of a sick cat by inserting a special stubby-ended thermometer into the anus, but the cat has strong sphincter muscles, which can make the procedure quite difficult. So, it is best only to attempt this at home under the specific direction of a veterinary surgeon.

NURSING A SICK CAT

While your cat may well need to be hospitalised at your vet's surgery for an operation or intensive nursing care, cats generally thrive best in surroundings that are familiar to them. Therefore your veterinary surgeon will probably be eager to return your cat to you as soon as possible. It is thus essential that you are clear about any specific directions that are given to you, and you should not hesitate to contact the surgery if you are unclear in any way. Administering medicines reliably is also extremely important – but sometimes easier said than done. The following guidelines should help you.

DEALING WITH WOUNDS

If your cat has had an operation, there is a strong chance that it will have a sutured wound. Cats do not tolerate bandages very well, so the stitches may be uncovered, and the cat is bound to lick at the wound. This does not usually do any harm, but if any stitches do come loose, then you should closely supervise the cat to try and prevent any more from being removed and visit the vet at the earliest opportunity. If the wound is gaping open it may well have to be resutured, so do not give your cat a meal before you visit the surgery, in case a general anaesthetic has to be given.

In some cases it is necessary to fit the cat with an Elizabethan collar, a wide plastic cone that fits over the neck and physically prevents the cat from worrying at a wound while still letting it eat and drink. These are not particularly popular with cats, especially when they first go on, but most cats eventually get used to them after a day or two. If your cat does come home complete with a bandage or a plaster, you should ensure that it is kept clean and dry. If you

notice an unpleasant smell, a lot of swelling or if the cat seems particularly uncomfortable, you should return to have the wound checked as a dressing that is too tight or becomes infected can do a lot more harm than good.

GIVING A TABLET

Grasp the cat's head firmly on either side of the jaw. Bend the head gently but firmly backwards until the lower jaw begins to drop open. Push the tablet on to the 'V' right at the back of the cat's throat.

THE ROLE OF TLC

Follow your vet's advice about letting your cat outdoors, which will almost certainly be inadvisable if it does have a dressing or plaster applied. After some operations it may be particularly important for your cat to rest and keep as still as possible. In these circumstances, confining the cat to a cage or a modified play-pen may be necessary, only taking your pet out to hold it on your lap and fuss over it.

Cats, like people, respond well to a large dose of that magic ingredient – Tender Loving Care. A warm bed, some tasty food (*see* chapter 5 for some recipes to tempt your ailing cat) and the company of their favourite person constitute the ideal prescription for a speedy recovery.

4

A – Z of
Aged Afflictions

The following chapter outlines the diseases that are most common in the elderly cat, and the chart opposite will help you to find the right part in the chapter if you are concerned about the health of your cat. By referring to the clinical signs on the left and answering the questions along the route, the chart will guide you to the section that is most likely to be relevant to your own cat. This is only a guide and is not a substitute for a proper veterinary examination. For your cat's sake, do not hesitate to obtain proper veterinary care if you are worried about its health.

AORTIC THROMBOSIS A thrombosis is the formation of a blood clot, which can block blood vessels. Clot formation is much more common in older animals and is often associated with a sluggish circulation due to heart disease (*see* heart disease). In aortic thrombosis, the clot forms in the lower part of the aorta, the main artery supplying blood to the cat's hind limbs. When the blood supply to the hind legs is suddenly cut off, the cat suffers acute pain due to muscle spasm in the hind-leg muscles, and the legs become completely paralysed.

Given time and painkillers, a new blood supply will often re-form and use of the legs will be regained. A very low dose of aspirin will help to prevent clots from re-forming, but this must only be given under veterinary direction as cats can easily be poisoned with this drug. Because the condition is so distressing, and it can be associated with an underlying heart problem, euthanasia is often recommended.

ANAEMIA To be anaemic is to have an abnormally low level of haemoglobin, the red oxygen-carrying pigment, in the blood. Anaemia is therefore not a disease in itself, but often a sign of an underlying problem. An examination of the size and haemoglobin content of the blood cells may help the veterinary surgeon to pinpoint which one of the many causes of anaemia is the particular problem. Anaemia can be caused by many factors, all of which decrease the haemoglobin content of the blood: blood loss; problems with the manufacture of new blood cells in the bone marrow: or excessive breakdown of the blood cells within the bloodstream. In the older cat, the most common triggers of anaemia, however, are kidney disease, infection with the feline leukaemia virus (*see* p.23) and tumours (*see* tumours) that affect the bone marrow. Some poisons, or even drugs given for specific disease, can also have an effect on the production of red blood cells. One type of anaemia, known as feline infectious anaemia, is caused by a parasite, *Haemobartonella felis* (the name will be changing to *Mycoplasma Haemofelis*), which attaches itself to the red blood cells and stimulates the host's body to destroy them. It is thought that the parasite is transmitted from one cat to another by biting insects such as fleas.

Cats with anaemia will tend to be dull and lethargic, and owners may notice that the gums lose their normal bright-pink colour and become paler, in severe cases even almost white. Diagnosis almost always involves a blood test to identify and treat the underlying cause of the problem. Sometimes it is necessary to take a sample of the bone marrow itself to see why it is not functioning properly. The cat will normally be sedated or given a light anaesthetic so that a needle can be introduced into the marrow cavity of a bone. This will suck out a sample of the marrow in order for the cells to be analysed under the microscope.

As well as treating the underlying disease, when possible extra minerals and vitamins, especially iron and vitamin B12, should be given to provide the building blocks that the body needs to manufacture new cells. In severe cases it is possible to give a blood transfusion from a donor cat, although currently this is infrequently carried out in veterinary practice.

ARTHRITIS This is an inflammation of one or more of the joints and can be caused by injury, excess of vitamin A or infection. In older animals it is usually a result of wear and tear on the joint over time. Fortunately, compared to other species, such as the dog, this condition is not common in cats, and because cats are relatively small and light they generally cope with it quite well if afflicted. Arthritis causes pain, swelling and stiffness in the joints, often seen as an unwillingness to jump normally. Many of the anti-inflammatory drugs that are used to treat arthritis in other species are poisonous to cats, so it is essential that any treatment is only given under the direction of a vet. There is no cure, but it is usually possible to control the problem effectively so that the cat can live a normal life.

BLINDNESS   The main causes of blindness in elderly cats are: injury to the eye itself; tumours affecting either the eye or the part of the brain that controls sight; cataracts; and diseases of the retina, the light-sensitive layer at the back of the eye.

A cataract is a clouding of the lens (situated behind the pupil in the centre of the eye) that invariably develops to some degree with age, although cataracts do not usually develop to the stage where the cat is completely blind. An injury to the eye or certain diseases, such as diabetes, can encourage cataracts to form. Although it is feasible to remove cataracts surgically, it would be unusual to carry out this procedure on an elderly cat.

A wide variety of diseases can affect the retina and cause blindness. In elderly cats, it is not uncommon for the retina to detach from the back of the eye, whereby it loses its blood supply and rapidly ceases to function, causing the pupil of the eye to become widely dilated. Another disease, glaucoma, involves a build-up of pressure within the eye itself, causing the whole eye to bulge; this can also damage the retina, but fortunately it is uncommon in cats.

It is obviously essential that any problem affecting the eye is treated promptly, before it becomes more serious and possibly sight-threatening. Watch out for swelling or redness around the eye, abnormal discharges, cloudiness of the cornea (the transparent front surface of the eye) or any indication that the cat is in pain or discomfort. Treatment will often involve putting drops or ointment into the eyes, so ensure you understand the directions properly and follow them to the letter. Your vet will show you how to put medication into the eye if you are unsure (*see* page 43, chapter 3).

Blindness in one eye is of very little consequence to a cat as they quickly learn to adapt to using the other eye alone. However, compared to the dog, which relies very much on its sense of smell, sight is very important to a cat, and many cats do not cope well with being entirely blind. Having said this, the older and less active cat will often manage quite well (*see* p.153, chapter 8).

BRONCHITIS *see* respiratory disease.

CANCER *see* tumours.

CONSTIPATION Constipation is common in elderly cats, due to a build-up of hard faeces within the rectum. Usually, the cat will strain to pass a motion, although in some cases it hardly seems to bother to try – it just stops eating and becomes generally unwell. Some constipated cats manage to pass small amounts of very liquid motions, which edge their way around the large, hard, compacted faeces sitting in the rectum.

Hair tends to bind the motions together and exacerbate the problem of constipation, and so elderly cats, which are moulting heavily, should be groomed regularly to prevent them swallowing large amounts of dead hair.

A teaspoon of liquid paraffin or similar laxative – a little cod liver oil or a commercial product such as Katalax – can be given to try and help the faeces pass through naturally. It is best to avoid laxatives on a regular basis as they tend to carry fat-soluble vitamins, such as vitamin A, out of the body, which can in turn cause deficiencies to develop. Bulking agents, for example Isogel or plain bran, can also be given to soften the motions on a long-term basis and thereby prevent recurrence. In the case of very severely constipated cats, an anaesthetic may be needed in order to administer an enema. This allows the veterinary surgeon to break up the faeces manually so they can pass out of the rectum.

If your cat is straining to go to the toilet, do take great care – especially in male cats – that the problem really is constipation and not a blockage to the flow of urine from the bladder. Such an obstruction to the flow of urine is an acute emergency, which requires immediate veterinary attention.

CONVULSIONS More commonly referred to as fits, convulsions are uncontrolled contractions and relaxations of the muscles, which result in uncoordinated 'paddling' movements of the legs. They can be caused by a whole range of underlying problems: brain tumours; certain poisons such as metaldehyde (slug bait); and diseases such as liver disorders, kidney failure or diabetes (see individual entries for these conditions). Some animals develop what is known as idiopathic epilepsy, when regular fits occur for no obvious reason, although sometimes an injury or previous illness may have been known to damage the brain. It is very uncommon for idiopathic epilepsy to develop in an elderly cat.

If a cat is having a fit, it is best to interfere with it as little as possible. Leave it in a dark and quiet place, ensuring that there is nothing around that is likely to cause injury. Most fits are over within a few minutes, although, if they persist for more than ten minutes, immediate veterinary assistance should be sought.

Once the fit has passed, the cat should be examined as soon as

possible by a vet to determine and treat the underlying cause of the convulsion. In cases where fits do not pass off by themselves, or when they keep recurring, it may be necessary to treat the cat with an anticonvulsant drug, designed to control the fits. If the underlying cause can be treated, then the course of drugs may be only temporary, but in many cases it is necessary to put the patient on permanent medication to control the problem. Once a cat has started treatment, it is essential that the drugs are given regularly and not stopped without veterinary advice, or very severe convulsions could result.

CUSHING'S DISEASE Also known as hyperadrenocorticalism, Cushing's disease is caused by an overproduction by the adrenal gland, a small gland situated just next to the kidneys, of steroid hormones in the body. This can be caused either by a tumour on the adrenal glands themselves, or by a tumour of the pituitary gland in the base of the brain, which controls the activity of the adrenals. It can also be caused by prolonged treatment with corticosteroid drugs, and it is more common in elderly cats. The disease causes great appetite and thirst, muscle wasting, a swollen abdomen and sometimes skin problems.

If excessive treatment with corticosteroids are causing the problem, then if possible the cat should be gradually weaned off them under close veterinary supervision. Surgical removal of either adrenal or pituitary tumours is very difficult, but it is sometimes possible to treat affected cats with a drug that selectively kills off adrenal tissue in order to reduce its output of steroid hormones.

CYSTITIS This condition is most commonly referred to as feline lower urinary tract disease, or feline urological syndrome, because it generally affects the whole of the lower urinary tract, rather than just the bladder, whereas cystitis is specifically an inflammation of the bladder. It is most commonly due to irritation caused by crystals that form in the urine. The crystals form around the element magnesium and prefer to grow in an alkaline urine. In some cases they can join together within the bladder to form an actual stone or a plug, which blocks the flow of urine down the urethra. The urethra is the tube that carries the urine from the bladder to the outside. Urinary obstruction is especially common in male cats where the urethra is quite narrow.

Cystitis affects cats of all ages, and once it has occurred there is a strong chance of later recurrence. An affected cat feels that it has to keep on passing urine, although only small amounts are passed each time. It will sometimes urinate in unusual places, such as down the plughole of the bath.

A cat with a blockage will strain rather as if it is constipated, but it is important to ensure that a 'constipated' cat is able to urinate normally, as a blockage to the urethra constitutes an emergency that requires immediate treatment. If the flow of urine from the bladder has been blocked, then an anaesthetic must be given, and a catheter passed to clear the obstruction. In some cases an X-ray may be required to show up larger stones in the bladder itself.

Most cats with uncomplicated cystitis will improve quickly with treatment – some even without. Increasing the cat's water intake is an essential part of trying to prevent the problem from recurring, so cutting out dry food may help. Your vet may well want to collect a urine sample to check for crystals, or signs of infection. Special veterinary diets are available to try and control urinary tract disease in cats, and your vet will be able to recommend the one best suited to your cat's needs.

DENTAL DISEASE Dental disease is extremely common in elderly cats and is usually caused by accumulation of hard, brown calculus on the teeth. This builds up gradually over the years and pushes on the gums to cause gingivitis, an inflammation of the gum tissue. Some cats seem to build up this deposit much more quickly than others, and diet can play a part in this process (*see* chapter 5). If left untreated, the gingivitis causes the gums to recede and form pockets, which then trap bacteria and become infected, thus weakening the lining that holds the tooth in its socket and eventually causing the tooth to become loose and drop out. Signs of dental problems include bad breath, redness and swelling of the gums and sometimes difficulty in eating food.

Other dental problems include broken teeth, which may then become infected, and erosion of the teeth, in which the crown of the tooth is eaten away until the tooth eventually breaks. The cause of this condition is not known, as cats do not seem to suffer from dental cavities, which are the cause of so many human fillings.

The sooner the dental disease is treated, the more chance there is of being able to preserve the teeth and avoid extraction. Tartar accumulation on the crown of the teeth alone may appear purely a cosmetic flaw, but as this can cause inflammation of the gums it should be removed. Some owners are reluctant to put an ageing cat through a general anaesthetic for relatively minor problems, but anaesthetics can now be given safely to even very elderly cats, and it is best to treat this problem before it becomes too severe.

A light anaesthetic is administered, and the teeth are descaled, usually using an ultrasonic descaler that shoots a spray of water particles, vibrating at a very high speed, on to the teeth. This shakes the tartar loose and washes it away. Badly infected teeth may need to be extracted. The surfaces of the good teeth are then smoothly polished to try and prevent the tartar building up again too quickly.

Cats are not able to tell us when their teeth are causing them pain or discomfort, but many owners report that their animals are much brighter after having had bad teeth attended to – even though the owners may not have realised that bad teeth were actually troubling their pet.

DIABETES MELLITUS Also known as sugar diabetes, diabetes mellitus is a disorder of the pancreatic gland, which is situated next to the stomach. The pancreas is responsible for producing the hormone insulin as well as digestive enzymes. Insulin controls the blood glucose levels, but in the condition of diabetes, the pancreas does not produce enough insulin and blood glucose levels rise. This, in turn, causes a build-up of poisons called ketones in the body, which damage vital organs, such as the liver, and can eventually cause the cat to lapse into a coma. Some cats develop diabetes mellitus in old age for no obvious reason, although in other cases it can be brought about by long-term treatment with such drugs as corticosteroids or certain steroid hormones. Obesity may also encourage the development of this condition.

A cat with diabetes mellitus initially develops an intensive thirst and excessive appetite, as it is unable to utilise the energy it is producing from the food that it eats. As the ketone levels build up in the blood, the cat becomes unwell and may go off its food. Ketones are related to acetone, and so an observant owner may notice that sickly sweet smell of nail-polish remover on the breath. In severe cases, the cat may start to have fits and go into a diabetic coma, and the outlook for successful treatment is much bleaker once the disease has developed to this stage. A urine test will readily show high levels of glucose in the urine, although glucose may be found in the urine of a cat that has just eaten a large meal or as a result of stress. The presence of ketones in the urine is diagnostic, but a blood test to measure blood glucose levels is usually used as a confirmation or if there are problems with collecting urine (*see* p. 43-44, chapter 3).

About 30 per cent of cats with diabetes can be controlled with oral medication, especially if it is started early in the course of the disease. The alternative is daily, or sometimes twice daily, injections with insulin. Many owners find the thought of injections terrifying, but a very fine needle is used, and it does not usually pose a problem after a few lessons from a member of the veterinary staff. In fact, in the long run, many owners find the injections easier than giving tablets. It is also important that the cat has regular feeding of similar amounts of food each day (*see* chapter 5 for further information on feeding) as the amount of insulin required to keep the blood glucose levels at the correct level varies with the amount of energy that the cat burns up and the amount of food that it eats.

Owners need to consider whether they can make satisfactory arrangements for the cat to have its injections if they are away, as treatment must be continued every day without fail. Some veterinary surgeries have the facility to board cats needing this type of treatment when owners are on holiday. Some catteries will also do it.

Urine samples have to be tested regularly to monitor glucose levels – this will initially be at least once a day, although it may be possible to do this less often once the amount of insulin that needs to be given each day has settled down to a predictable level. Using special litter trays with drainage channels and non-absorbent cat litter makes life easier. In addition, simple testing strips are available so that owners can check the urine ketone and glucose levels simply by dipping the stick into the urine sample, waiting the allotted time and then matching the colour of the strip to the colour chart on the side of the pack.

Initially, the vet will give the daily injections of insulin, starting at a low dose and gradually building up the amount given until the desired effect is achieved. Some vets like to hospitalise their patients to achieve this, but since returning home upsets the routine that has been established and thus the requirement for insulin, many vets prefer to treat all but the most advanced cases on an outpatient basis. There is a risk that the blood glucose levels could fall too low, which would cause a hypoglycaemic convulsion – a fit caused by low blood-sugar levels starving the brain of energy. This is particularly likely if insulin is given when the cat is off its food, so it is best to feed a meal before giving the daily insulin injection and contact the vet about reducing the dose given if the cat does not eat for any reason. It is also wise to have some glucose powder to hand, as this can be quickly dissolved in water and given by mouth if the cat shows any sign of becoming weak or twitchy because of low blood glucose levels.

Regular veterinary check-ups are essential to monitor the diabetic cat and to watch out for signs of secondary problems due to the disease. The commonest complication in cats is blindness, either due to the developments of cataracts (see p.50), or damage to the small blood vessels in the light-sensitive retina at the back of the eye. Liver disease can also develop, leading to digestive upsets and eventually a loss of appetite.

All this may sound pretty daunting to the cat owner faced with deciding whether to embark on a course of treatment for a diabetic cat, and, in some cases, circumstances do not make treatment a realistic option and the cat has to be put to sleep. However, diabetic cats are not uncommon, and many owners manage to stabilise their cats very successfully on daily insulin injections. Diabetic cats can often live for at least two years after treatment is started, and sometimes considerably longer.

DIGESTIVE UPSETS As a cat ages, its digestive system becomes less able to cope with a rich or unbalanced diet. Over the years, most owners become aware of the sort of foods that suit their own cat, and those that seem to precipitate problems – for example many cats get diarrhoea if they eat liver, while others seem unable to tolerate milk. Some cats that have been fed on canned foods throughout their lives do not seem to digest them properly when they get older. Therefore they have to be changed to a fresh, bland diet to avoid repeated digestive upsets, which can manifest themselves as vomiting or diarrhoea – or, if you are really unlucky, a combination of both. Of course, vomiting and diarrhoea can also be signs of more generalised problems such as liver or kidney disease (*see* hepatitis, jaundice, kidney disease).

If a cat vomits, food should be withheld for 24 hours, and the cat encouraged to drink small amounts of water little and often. Rehydration powders, designed to be added to water, supply glucose and extra minerals and are available from vets. Once the vomiting has settled, a bland diet, such as white fish or chicken, should be fed in small quantities. A cat that is vomiting repeatedly or is very much off colour should be seen by a vet without delay, as dehydration and shock can set in very rapidly and fluid replacement by means of an intravenous drip is sometimes necessary.

Diarrhoea is generally less likely to be life-threatening, and it is worth trying a light diet for a couple of days, possibly combined with a teaspoon of kaolin twice daily (available from a chemist) to see if it settles, provided, of course, that the cat is not showing any other serious signs of being unwell. Any change back to a normal diet should be made gradually by mixing increasing proportions of their regular food into the bland diet over a few days. If the problem recurs, the cat should be put back on to the light diet for a longer period.

EAR DISEASE Chronic ear infections are common in cats of any age, and in some cases they can spread from the outer ear down to the organ of balance in the inner ear (*see* loss of balance). Older cats quite often develop growths within the ear canal, which then cause a build-up of discharge and infection. These growths are not usually cancerous, and it is possible to carry out an operation to open out the side wall of the ear canal and remove the growth. This operation, called an aural resection, is also used to improve the ventilation to the ear canal in cases of chronic infection, particularly when the ear canal has become narrowed as a result of long-term inflammation.

Deafness is not uncommon in elderly cats and is usually due to a degeneration of the hearing apparatus deep down in the ear. There is usually no treatment for the condition, and indeed owners often take a long time to realise their cat is deaf – the majority of cats tend to ignore the calls of their owner most of the time anyway! The main danger is that cats become unable to hear oncoming traffic, and so deaf cats should preferably be kept indoors or in an enclosed garden (*see* chapter 8).

FITS *see* convulsions.

HEART DISEASE Heart disease that is present from birth, such as a 'hole in the heart', is very rare in cats and, if serious, would have caused problems when the cat was young. Dogs are very prone to degeneration of the valves of the heart in old age, but this is also quite rare in cats.

The most common type of heart disease in cats is cardiomyopathy, a degeneration of the heart muscle. It has been discovered that many cases can be caused by a deficiency of the amino acid taurine in the diet, and proprietary cat foods now have booster taurine levels to prevent the problem. In many other cases the cause in unknown, although it can also be associated with hyperthyroidism (*see* hyperthyroidism).

The failing heart muscle is not able to pump the blood properly around the body, and this most commonly leads to an accumulation of fluid on the lungs and severe breathing problems. It can also cause acute paralysis of the hind limbs due to aortic thrombosis (*see* aortic thrombosis). The condition can often be diagnosed by radiography, although it may be necessary to drain off some of the fluid from the chest first so that the heart outline can be more clearly seen. More sophisticated techniques, such as ultrasound examination, may also be useful in some cases.

Diuretic drugs, which prevent the accumulation of fluid on the chest, taken with drugs to slow down the heart rate, thin the blood and reduce clotting often bring about an improvement. If a dietary deficiency is suspected, then a supplement can be fed. However, the underlying deterioration of the heart muscle cannot be reversed once it develops, and the long-term outlook for cats with this condition is not good.

HEPATITIS The liver is the processing factory of the body, and hepatitis is an inflammation of the liver, which can be caused by a variety of factors such as the ingestion of poisons, infectious agents or simply scarring of the liver tissue with wear and tear (known as cirrhosis). Affected cats will generally become listless and inappetent, and very prone to stomach upsets as the liver plays a major part in the digestion of food.

Sometimes the underlying cause can be treated, for example by stopping the administration of any drugs that may be affecting the liver or by giving antibiotics in the case of a bacterial infection. The liver does have a great ability to regenerate itself. In other cases it is only possible to support the liver by the feeding of a low-fat, easily digested diet plus a dietary supplement rich in the B vitamins and the amino acid methionine, which has been shown to help liver function.

HYPERTHYROIDISM Hyperthyroidism is an overactivity of the thyroid gland and is extremely common in older cats, although the cause is not known. The two thyroid glands are situated in the neck to either side and below the larynx, or voice box. They can not normally be felt at all, but when they enlarge and cause this condition they can usually be felt by an experienced hand. This enlargement is usually non-cancerous, although in rare cases it can be caused by a malignant growth.

The thyroid gland can be thought of as the accelerator pedal of the body, and the hormone that it produces controls the rate of metabolism. Therefore a hyperthyroid cat is furiously burning up energy, typically making it overactive, over hungry and excessively thirsty. Despite its voracious appetite the cat becomes very thin, and all the energy that it consumes usually makes it very keyed-up and nervy, with a racing heartbeat. Some cats become incontinent indoors or vomit their food. In the later stage of the disease, the heart is often damaged by having to beat so fast, and the cat may become dull and lose its appetite. If left untreated, the cat usually dies of heart failure.

The symptoms of excessive thirst and loss of weight can often make an owner suspect kidney disease, but the condition is easily diagnosed by a blood test to measure the thyroid hormone levels. The outlook for this condition is much better than for kidney disease. Many owners bring their elderly, thin cat to the vet expecting that it will have to be put to sleep and are delighted to discover that their much loved pet can be given a new lease of life with treatment.

There are three treatments available for this condition:

1) Anti-thyroid drugs are usually given initially to bring down the level of thyroid hormones, and can be given at a reduced dose in the long term. Some cats are impossible to medicate orally, or develop side effects from treatment, such as lethargy and swollen lymph glands, and then alternatives have to be used.

2) Once drugs have been used to bring the condition under control, one or both thyroid glands can be removed surgically. This should only be carried out once the cat has had a repeat blood test to show that its thyroid hormone levels have come down to an acceptable level, and that its kidney function is still in order. Great care has to be taken to prevent damage to the parathyroid glands, which are closely associated with the thyroids. They control calcium levels in the blood and are essential for life. Surprisingly, many cats that have had both thyroid glands removed do not require oral thyroid hormone supplementation.

3) The cat can be injected with a radioactive isotope of iodine, which will kill off the thyroid tissue without damaging other organs. This avoids the need for an anaesthetic, and is particularly useful when the thyroid-producing cells are situated within the chest cavity and hard to reach surgically. The beauty of the treatment is its safety and simplicity. The problem is that the cat becomes radioactive for several weeks after the treatment has been given, and has to be kept in a special isolation unit, with all its waste products disposed off as radioactive waste. Several such units now exist in the UK.

INCONTINENCE This can be urinary incontinence or faecal incontinence, or possibly a combination of both. Obviously, urinary tract disorders such as cystitis (*see* cystitis) could cause a normally clean cat to urinate indoors, and likewise diarrhoea (*see* digestive upsets) may result in a cat defecating indoors. Any problem that causes the cat to drink excessively may also mean that it is not able to control its urination if it is shut indoors for any length of time. If a veterinary examination does not suggest a medical problem as the cause of the incontinence, then it may be due to psychological reasons (*see* chapter 6).

JAUNDICE Jaundice is a build-up of pigments in the skin and other tissues, causing a yellow discoloration, which is most visible in the whites of the eyes. These bile pigments, as they are called, are produced by the breakdown of the red blood pigment haemoglobin and are processed by the liver, before being excreted via the bile duct and gall bladder into the intestines.

Jaundice can be caused by an excessive breakdown of red blood cells (such as is caused by feline infectious anaemia – *see* anaemia), disease of the liver itself or obstruction to the flow of bile out of the body. In the first instance, stools will often be darker than normal because of a high bile content, whereas in the case of an obstruction the faeces will usually be much lighter then normal.

Gallstones are a frequent cause of jaundice in humans but are very rare in cats. The commonest causes of jaundice in the elderly cat are liver tumours, which carry a very poor prognosis, or lymphocytic cholangitis, an inflammation of the bile ducts within the liver that causes a gross enlargement of that organ. The cause of the latter disease is not known, but some cases can be controlled quite well with large doses of anti-inflammatory drugs. Even once the underlying cause of the jaundice has been removed, it may take several weeks before the yellow discoloration fades.

KIDNEY DISEASE There are many different ways in which the kidneys of an older cat can become diseased and, although the external signs of illness may be very similar for all of them, the treatment required differs markedly. The commonest cause is a scarring of the kidney tissue, which develops slowly over the years. Tumours of the kidney are also very common in old age and usually result from exposure to infection by the feline leukaemia virus earlier on in life. Another more unusual form of kidney disease is that caused by damage to the glomeruli, the parts of the kidney that actually filter the blood to produce urine. When these are damaged, they allow protein from the blood to leak out into the urine, resulting in a very low protein level in the blood. This results in a build-up of fluid under the skin, known as subcutaneous oedema. Occasionally stones may form in the kidneys, although this is much more common lower down in the urinary tract, for example in the bladder.

The earliest signs of kidney disease are increased urine production, because the kidneys are not able to concentrate the urine properly, and an increase in drinking (recognising this can be tricky, *see* p.41-42). These are followed by gradual loss of weight and body condition, until eventually the cat goes off its food and, in the terminal stages, ceases drinking entirely.

The kidneys are responsible for removing waste products from the body, particularly urea, a by-product of protein digestion. In the later stages of kidney failure, urea levels build up in the blood, further damaging the body organs, making the cat feel unwell and causing a somewhat unpleasant smell to the breath. There is also a tendency for a cat with kidney disease to lose excessive amounts of calcium in the urine and retain phosphorus in the blood, which can result in a softening of the bones.

Many owners do not recognise the warning signs of kidney disease until it is very advanced, and the cat has gone off its food. But, even the earliest warning signs are not seen until over two-thirds of the functioning kidney tissue has been damaged. Nevertheless, the outlook is much brighter if it can be diagnosed as soon as possible, but the diagnosis of kidney disease depends upon the cat's symptoms, combined with the results of a blood test. A urine test will measure the protein levels in the urine, and the concentration of the urine itself is also very useful. If you suspect kidney disease, it is helpful to take a urine sample along with you when you visit the vet. Taking an X-ray may help if the vet suspects the problem is a tumour or kidney stones. It is also possible to inject a special dye into the blood, which will outline the internal structure of the kidneys on an

X-ray, or ultimately to take a biopsy specimen of the kidney tissue itself with a special needle that can be passed, under anaesthetic, through a small incision in the abdomen.

The exact line of treatment depends upon the underlying cause of the disease. Kidney stones can be surgically removed or dissolved with a special diet. However, most elderly cats with kidney disease suffer from scarring of the tissue and, since nothing can be done to repair this, treatment depends upon helping the cat to cope as well as possible with the functioning kidney tissue that it has available and upon trying to minimise any further damage.

As the main signs of illness result from a build-up of urea and phosphorus in the blood, much can be achieved by switching to a diet that has moderately restricted protein and phosphorus levels. This is complicated when too much protein is being lost by the kidneys, and in such cases higher protein levels have to be fed despite their harmful effect. It should be stressed that this is quite rare, and that by and large the treatment of kidney disease involves feeding a low-protein diet. Drugs such as anabolic steroids can also be given to help the weight loss that occurs, and extra vitamins, especially of the B group, should be fed to replace those lost.

More recently, a group of drugs called ACE inhibitors, which reduce blood pressure, have been found to make a significant difference to the length and quality of life of cats affected by kidney disease, and are now becoming widely used. Nursing plays a large part in the treatment of kidney disease. A cat that is acutely ill with kidney failure will need intensive treatment if it is to stand a chance of getting over the initial crisis. Such treatment includes giving intravenous fluid therapy to flush out the toxins from the body and correct the dehydration that inevitably occurs. A very fine tube passed down the nose enables liquid food to be passed directly into the cat's stomach.

A careful decision has to be made in consultation with the veterinary surgeon to consider if this form of intensive treatment is worthwhile – each case must be judged on its own merits (see chapter 9, on euthanasia). For the more chronic cases, the main difficulty is persuading the cat to eat what is best for it. The earlier in the course of the disease the diet is adjusted, the more chance there is of success, as the last thing a seriously ill cat wants is a change to its diet. Most cats prefer a diet that is very high in protein, and various tricks have to be used to encourage them to eat (see chapter 5, on special needs). Special diets are available from your veterinary surgeon, and if your cat will eat them they provide the ideal balance of protein and other nutrients. If your cat refuses to eat them, you may have to resort to concocting your own recipes (see chapter 5, pp. 85-86).

Unless the problem has been picked up in its very early stages, the long-term outlook for a cat with kidney disease is somewhat bleak, as around two-thirds of the kidney tissue will have been irreparably damaged. Having said this, some cats take very well to treatment, and even some quite advanced cases can live a happy life for two or three more years.

LIVER DISEASE *see* hepatitis; jaundice.

LOSS OF BALANCE Loss of balance is usually due either to a deep ear infection, which passes from the outer ear across the eardrum and affects the organ of balance within the inner part of the ear, or to a 'stroke', which is more common in the elderly cat. Strictly speaking, cats do not suffer from the same sort of strokes that commonly affect humans, but nevertheless they are affected by a sudden severance of the blood supply to the parts of the brain that control the sense of balance, and this has a very similar result.

In either case, the cat will suddenly lose its sense of balance, may circle continually in one direction or even lose its ability to stand entirely. In milder cases, or during the recovery stages, the cat may simply tilt its head to one side. In elderly cats, brain tumours can also cause similar symptoms, although the onset is usually more gradual. If an interruption to the blood supply has caused the problem, it often improves with time and, although many cats are left with a permanent tilt to the head, they usually adapt to it very well. The outlook for a cat with a brain tumour is obviously much poorer, although in some cases drug treatment can give the cat a very useful lease of life.

If an ear infection is present, this can often be treated with antibiotics. In some very deep-seated cases, however, it may be necessary to resort to surgery to drain any accumulated pus from the bony chambers deep in the ear canal.

OBESITY Cats are generally quite good at adjusting their food intake to match their requirements and, although they do tend to become a little portly after neutering, it is quite rare for a cat to become so fat that it seriously affects its health. This is fortunate because it is quite difficult to adjust the calorie intake of most cats as they often refuse to eat higher-fibre, reduced-calorie diets, and they raid the local dustbins to make up for what they perceive as any deficits in their intake. It is easier to control the food consumption of indoor cats, but a hungry cat is very capable of making the life of its owner pure hell until it gets the quantity and quality of food it demands!

Regular weighing will soon confirm whether your cat is putting on weight, and it is far easier to make minor adjustments to the diet early on, and thus prevent obesity, than to attempt crash diets at a later stage to get the weight off a fat cat. Overweight cats are also very efficient at maintaining their body weight, as they tend to be very inactive and have a very effective insulating layer of fat around them to conserve their body heat.

Overweight cats should not be fed on ordinary dry cat foods, as they have a much higher calorie content than canned foods (but special low-calorie, dry cat foods are available). In order to achieve weight loss without the cat noticing it too much, it is advisable to increase the fibre content of the food and keep the level of fat relatively low (*see* chapter 5).

OVERACTIVE THYROID *see* hyperthyroidism.

OVERGROWN NAILS The toenails of a cat are not solid like those of a dog, but multilayered like an onion. They do not wear down as the cat walks as they are normally kept retracted, and the outer layer is pulled off when the cat scratches on a post to expose the new, sharp nail underneath. It is preferable to avoid clipping the nails of young and active cats as they need to keep them sharp for hunting, climbing and self-defence (it is always someone else's cat that does the attacking!), and they do tend to splinter if cut.

However, toenails do sometimes overgrow in elderly cats, and even though they may have a suitable scratching-post available, they may not be bothered to use it. In mild cases, this may simply result in the cat continually snagging its claws in fabric, but in advanced cases the nail can actually grow right round in a circle and back into the toe itself, causing severe pain and inflammation. The nails of an elderly cat should be regularly checked, and the ends clipped back if necessary.

PARALYSIS Compared to the situation in dogs, where paralysis of the hind limbs is all too common due to disc problems in the long-backed breeds, this condition is quite rare in cats and is most commonly the result of a road accident. However, a blockage to the blood vessels of the hind limbs can also cause paralysis (*see* aortic thrombosis), and this can be treated as a medical condition. In the older cat, tumours of the spine do occur from time to time, and in most cases surgical removal is not possible.

Wheeled carts to support the hind legs can be quite successful in dogs and have been tried for cats. However, because the cat is such an active animal and enjoys jumping so much more than a dog, their use is probably not justified, and euthanasia is a kinder alternative.

PARASITES The categories of parasites that affect the cat can be divided into external parasites, which live on the skin, and internal parasites, which live within the body. Neither is a particular problem for older cats, although each can take advantage of a debilitated animal and cause concern. Prevention is always better than cure, so it is advisable to treat your cat regularly with a flea preparation throughout the year and to worm it at least every six months – more often if you see any sign of the long, stringy roundworms or the flat, rice-like, tapeworm segments. The most effective products for the control of parasites are available from your veterinary surgeon.

PHARYNGITIS Pharyngitis is an inflammation of the throat

and may be seen in combination with gingivitis, an inflammation of the gums (*see* dental disease). Many irritants and infections can cause an inflammation within the mouth, and the ailment may well stem from a problem with the teeth. However, some animals with perfectly healthy teeth develop a very severe and persistent sore mouth to the point at which the cat is not able to cope with eating.

Sometimes a growth in the back of the throat can make it look as if it is badly inflamed, but many of these cases have been shown to be due to infection with either the feline leukaemia virus or the feline immunodeficiency virus. If the inflammation is very bad, the cat can be blood tested for these viruses, and a small sample of tissue taken from the throat if necessary. Some cases respond to a long course of antibiotic treatment, others to anti-inflammatory drugs, but this is a very difficult problem to cure entirely, and treatment all too often consists of control rather than cure.

RENAL DISEASE *see* kidney disease.

RESPIRATORY DISEASE Many different conditions can affect the respiratory system of the elderly cat, such as an accumulation of fluid around the lungs due to heart disease. It is also quite common for tumours, particularly cancers that have spread from other parts of the body, to affect the lungs.

Probably the most common condition to affect the lungs of elderly cats is chronic bronchitis, a long-standing infection of the tubes that connect the upper airways to the lungs themselves. This infection tends to cause a persistent, hacking cough. Cats with this problem are usually perfectly well in themselves but have bouts of violent coughing that most owners find particularly distressing. A chest X-ray is probably advisable to rule out other problems, and treatment usually consists of a long course of antibiotics to clear the infection as thoroughly as possible. In some cases, the veterinary surgeon may want to pass a fine tube down into the chest under anaesthetic and take some samples. Cell types will then be examined to find out which particular antibiotic is likely to be most effective on the existing bacteria.

RHINITIS Rhinitis is an inflammation of the lining of the nose. It may be due to the cat-flu virus infection or a foreign body that has entered the nostril. If it involves the bony chambers in the skull that connect to the main nasal chambers, it is more correctly called a sinusitis. In older cats it is often seen as 'snuffles', so called because the cat continually snuffles and sneezes, often with a discharge from the nostrils. Often this will have been caused by a severe respiratory infection earlier on in life, which has permanently damaged the lining of the nose. It can also be due to fungal infections or tumours growing within the nose. Some cats with chronic infections of the deeper parts of the ear can get polyps. These grow from the middle ear and down the tiny Eustachian tube, which connects the ear with the back of the throat, and enlarge in that position, causing similar signs to a chronic rhinitis.

Antibiotics will usually be used as the first line of attack, although a long course of treatment may be necessary in well-established cases. Examination of the throat under anaesthetic and an X-ray of the nose are advisable if there is not a good response to treatment, in order to rule out any other causes of the problem. But, even some cases of straightforward infection do tend to keep recurring after therapy.

SINUSITIS *see* rhinitis.

SKIN DISEASE Elderly cats are prone to the same range of skin diseases that might affect a younger cat. Flea allergies, in particular, are very common, causing either scabby patches known as miliary dermatitis, or bald patches where the cat has worn the hair away by constant licking. Skin tumours are quite rare in the cat, although cats with white ears are particularly prone to squamous cell carcinomas of the ear flaps, a cancerous growth that results from repeated bouts of sunburn on unprotected skin.

Problems with the coat itself are more common in those elderly cats less able or willing to maintain the regular grooming that the coat needs to remain healthy. Arthritis in the joints of the neck or a sore mouth (*see* pharyngitis) may contribute towards this reluctance. Even a short-haired cat that has coped with grooming itself throughout its life may need assistance with regular grooming in old age, and if the coat becomes severely matted it may be necessary for your vet to comb or cut out the knots under sedation or light anaesthesia.

A nutritious diet will help to maintain coat quality in later life, and a balanced vitamin and mineral supplement could well be added to the normal diet. Evening primrose oil is particularly useful for improving coat quality as it is very rich in the essential fatty acid gamma linolenic acid (GLA), and there is some evidence to suggest that many older cats are less able to absorb sufficient quantities of fatty acids from their food.

STROKES *see* loss of balance.

TUMOURS Tumours is a very broad category used to describe growths that can be divided into benign tumours, which generally grow slowly and do not spread to other parts of the body, and malignant tumours, or cancers. Cancer is a highly emotive term but, just as many forms of cancer in humans can now be successfully treated, the same is true with cats. Tumours are generally more common in older cats, and if cancers do develop in young animals they tend to be aggressive and more difficult to treat.

The commonest cancer in the cat is lymphosarcoma, or cancer of the white blood cells, because it is often triggered by infection with the feline leukaemia virus (*see* chapter 3). This can take several forms. In the young cat, it often affects the thymus gland in the chest, causing a build-up of fluid in the chest and severe breathing problems. In older animals it most commonly affects the various lymph glands around the body, causing them to swell up enormously, or the white blood cells in the blood and bone marrow, resulting in a condition very similar to human leukaemia. Squamous cell carcinoma, a form of skin cancer, is also quite common in the cat, especially on the ears of white-coated cats due to chronic sunburn, or in and around the mouth.

Thankfully, breast cancer is rare in cats because spaying is so common, although it can occur when cats are given long-term hormone treatment. There are many other forms of cancer, which can affect just about any part of the body – many a veterinary textbook has been written on just this one subject.

Early diagnosis is vital if a tumour is to be treated successfully, so don't delay in taking your cat to the vet if you feel any unusual lumps or bumps. Benign tumours can be surgically excised, or even left alone if they are small and not interfering with body function. If there is any doubt about their nature, the surgeon will often send off a piece of tumour tissue to a laboratory for examination under the microscope. Some cancerous tumours lend themselves well to surgical treatment, but it is important to remove all the tumour in one go if at all possible, or the remaining cancer cells will grow even more quickly.

Radiotherapy is available in some treatment centres in the United Kingdom, and this is particularly useful for squamous cell carcinomas, which cannot be entirely removed. Lymphosarcoma is particularly amenable to chemotherapy (treatment with anti-cancer drugs). Whereas, in humans, very intensive courses of treatment are given to try and effect a lifetime cure, in cats the aim is to give lower doses to achieve a good period of remission without any serious side-effects. Cats with this disease will usually die within a matter of weeks if left untreated, while, with treatment, many cats have lived perfectly happy lives for two or more years. Just as the diagnosis of cancer is no longer the automatic death sentence that it used to be for humans, there is now much that can be done for cats with malignant tumours, either to cure the problem or to give them a useful extra lease of life.

5

Feline Cuisine

The basic principles of feeding for health early in life have been dealt with in chapter 2, and the same basic guidelines apply in old age. However, as a cat ages, its nutritional demands may well change. Older cats are often more finicky with the foods that they will eat, choosing to eat little and often. Overall, they will tend to eat less, because they are not as active as they were when they were young. Many older cats also have rather fewer teeth than in their younger days and will therefore find it difficult to eat hard food, or food that requires a lot of tearing and chewing, such as lumps of raw meat (of course, if a cat has a sore mouth, it should receive veterinary attention – *see* chapter 4: dental disease; pharyngitis).

FOOD, GLORIOUS FOOD!

A great deal of research has gone into studying the dietary needs of older cats and, as a result, there are now several ranges of food designed specifically to meet their requirements. There are several age-related changes that may have a bearing on the diet that an elderly cat is fed:

- Older cats tend to lose body weight as they age because they utilise their food less effectively. Therefore, most elderly cats need a diet that contains higher levels of easily digested energy than a younger one. Cats digest fat particularly well, so diets for elderly cats tend to contain higher levels of fat.

- Older cats have a higher requirement for certain fatty acids in their diet, to help maintain proper function on their nervous and immune systems. Adding the correct type of fat to their diet will ensure that older cats receive enough of these nutrients.

- As the senses become duller in older animals, they need a diet that is more highly palatable than that required by a young cat. If a cat is unable to smell a food, it will almost certainly refuse to eat it.

- As meat-eating animals, cats require relatively high levels of protein in their diet. There is no direct evidence to prove that this plays a part in causing kidney disease, but this condition is certainly amongst the most common in the ageing cat. Many have sub-clinical kidney disease, which means that their kidney function is abnormal without any obvious external signs. In these cases, providing a diet that contains moderate amounts of good quality protein, and limited amounts of phosphorus (which tends to build up in the body of cats suffering from the condition), will slow down the progression of the disease. Therefore, most diets for elderly cats are designed in this way as a preventative measure.

• Dental disease is extremely common in older cats. Special diets can help to exercise the teeth and gums with a special fibre structure that helps to remove accumulated tartar. If the mouth is sore, or many teeth have been extracted, the cat may not be able to manage to eat normal dry foods, and will need to be offered a senior diet with a smaller, softer, kibble, or put onto moist foods.

• Older cats have a higher requirement for certain vitamins and minerals than younger cats, although they must never be given to excess, as they may then cause more harm than good. Substances called antioxidants have been shown to help slow down the process of cell damage that accelerates as the cat gets older, and so they are boosted in diets for elderly cats. Similarly, the amino acid called carnitine has been shown to be beneficial to the elderly.

• Cats are very prone to urinary problems at all stages of their life, and maintenance diets are designed to produce a slightly acidic urine to reduce the incidence of a certain type of crystal, called struvite, that forms in the urine. These crystals can cause irritation, which leads to cystitis, or, in males cats, can even cause a blockage. Older cats are more prone to a different type of crystal, called oxalate, and unlike struvite, this tends to form in acidic urine. Therefore, diets for elderly cats are designed to produce more alkaline urine than those for younger ones.

Having said this, the ideal diet for a healthy, older cat need not vary hugely from a young adult's, so if all is well you can continue to feed a balanced diet, such as one of the complete canned or dry cat foods. However, dietary management plays an important part in the control of many ailments, and some older cats will have special feeding requirements relating to a specific problem.

Commercially produced diets are now available from veterinary surgeries for various conditions and diseases and if your cat accepts them, they are designed to provide the ideal balance of nutrients to control a particular problem while still providing all normal maintenance requirements. Any change of diet should be gradual, mixing the new food in increasing proportions over several days, or stomach upsets could result. There are several things you can do to tempt your cat to eat a particular food.

- Warm the food slightly, as cats are hunters in the wild and like to eat their food at body temperature
- Mix in small amounts of highly palatable food, such as liver, until your cat gets used to the new food (but do check first with your veterinary surgeon)
- Hand feed the food
- Prepare the food in small amounts – small cans are better than large ones. The act of opening a can seems to excite the tastebuds of cats
- Increase the fat content, as cats find fat very tasty. For example some of the kidney diets below are quite firm and can be sliced and lightly fried in oil

SPECIAL NEEDS

The principles of dietary management for various diseases are listed below, but if you would prefer to prepare some *haute cuisine* for your cat, or if your cat has you so well trained that it will accept nothing less, a recipe section is included at the end of this chapter.

KIDNEY DISEASE

Many of the clinical signs of kidney disease come from an accumulation of waste products produced by the breakdown of protein in the body, which, combined with a loss of calcium and a build-up of phosphorus, damage the kidneys. A change in diet is one of the most useful measures that can be taken to improve the condition of the cat and slow down further deterioration, because once kidney tissue is scarred it cannot regenerate. The sooner that the diet is changed in the course of the disease the better as, once the cat becomes unwell and grows more picky with its food, the less chance there is of getting it to accept a new diet. The cat with a kidney disease needs to be fed a diet with restricted levels of protein, phosphorus and salt, and with extra B vitamins. It is important that the correct balance of protein is given, since cats have a much higher requirement for protein than other species. Protein levels cannot be reduced too low. Cats will generally not accept a lot of starchy foods in their diet, but as they are very keen on fat, a high-fat diet will provide the energy a cat with kidney disease needs without excess levels of protein. Given the choice, cats will eat a diet that is very high in protein. However, by introducing fatty foods, such as unsalted bacon rind, and starchy foods, such as potatoes and pasta, as some 50 per cent of the diet, and by feeding good quality meat or fish for the other half, with a yeast-based B vitamin supplement, a cat with kidney problems will improve without running the risk of protein deficiency.

Several manufacturers make pre-prepared diets for cats with kidney disease, and in this way you can be certain that you are giving the ideal balance of nutrients for your cat. These foods come canned or in dry form, and it is worth trying both with fussy cats, as some will refuse one but enthusiastically tuck into the other. Some of the canned foods are quite dry, and palatability can be improved by dicing into chunks and very lightly frying in oil. You can aid the transition to the new diet by mixing in some of your cat's favourite foods, but in the long term you should aim to feed just the prescribed diet.

OBESITY

Cats are better at adjusting their food intake to their needs than us humans, but nevertheless obesity can be a problem, particularly in the older and less active cat. Simply reducing the amount of food given can be a problem, as the cat will just go out and raid the neighbourhood or drive its poor owners demented until they give in and offer some more food.

Dried cat foods are more calorie-dense than canned or fresh foods, and so should not be fed to overweight cats unless specifically designated low calorie. Increasing the fibre content of the food to make the cat feel that its stomach is full will encourage the cat to take in less calories. Again, proprietary low-calorie cat foods are now available, although a similar effect can be achieved by adding some wheat bran to the food. Even the most greedy of cats will only tolerate about a level teaspoon of bran in each bowl of food. Regular weighing is extremely useful to pick up fluctuations in body weight.

CONSTIPATION

Constipation is another problem that will usually respond to a high-fibre diet to soften the motions. Hair will tend to bind the faeces, so regular grooming to remove as much dead hair as possible is essential. Laxatives such as liquid paraffin can be used to lubricate the passage of the motions, but repeated use can lead to a deficiency of the fat-soluble vitamins such as vitamin A.

DIABETES

Cats tend to eat a relatively low amount of carbohydrate, and the problem of excessive levels of sugar in the diet does not generally arise. Diabetics need a very stable diet so that insulin requirements do not fluctuate too much, and a high-fibre content to slow down the absorption of digested food through the bowel. This will also help to avoid obesity and can be achieved by feeding one of the prescription diets designed for weight control, although a higher-energy food may be necessary if the cat is underweight.

DIARRHOEA AND/OR VOMITING

Cats with digestive upsets are generally best starved for 24 hours, and then put on to a light diet, which is low in fat. White meat or white fish with a little carbohydrate, such as boiled rice, is best and should be fed little and often. No attempt should be made to feed an ordinary diet until the problem has thoroughly cleared, and then the change should be made gradually over a few days. Some cats seem unable to digest commercial cat foods and have to be kept on a fresh meat diet. Special veterinary diets are now available to feed cats that have difficulty digesting normal foods.

CAT FLU

The sense of smell is crucial to the cat, and they will often refuse to eat food if they are not able to smell it because of a blocked-up nose. Cats suffering from cat flu may also have a sore mouth, so they are best fed on soft, smelly foods, such as freshly prepared, mashed-up sardines in oil. Warming the food slightly will increase the aroma and placing a little into the mouth on a finger (but don't get bitten!) may stimulate interest in the food. Special liquid diets are now made for cats that are not able to cope with solid food.

FEEDING AFTER SURGERY

Follow closely the directions given by your veterinary surgeon in the period immediately after an operation. In some cases, cats may be able to have a light meal on the evening after an anaesthetic, but, in other cases, particularly after surgery on the bowel, it may be necessary to withhold food for some time – your vet will advise you on this.

The same principles of feeding outlined above for an animal suffering from cat flu may also be applied to nursing after an operation. Sometimes, it may be necessary to force-feed a liquid food with a syringe, by gently holding back the cat's head and slowly dribbling the food into the mouth. But great care must be taken to give the food slowly so that it is not inhaled into the lungs, as this can start up a pneumonia and cause a lot more harm than good. Balanced semi-liquid foods for cats are now available from your vet for just this purpose.

Cats that are unwilling or not able to eat for an extended period can be hospitalised and fed either with a tube that is inserted under a light anaesthetic to enter the gullet through a skin incision in the side of the neck and then into the stomach, or by passing a very fine tube through one nostril and down into the stomach. Both these means of feeding are tolerated surprisingly well by most cats.

URINARY PROBLEMS
Irritation of the bladder and sometimes even blockage of the urethra, the tube that carries urine out from the bladder can occur in cats (*see* cystitis, chapter 4).

CATERING FOR YOUR CAT
While prepared foods are now available to provide a well-balanced diet for any cat, many owners gain a lot of satisfaction from cooking for their cat, aided by the antics of their pet rubbing itself around their legs while their gourmet dinner is being prepared. All the recipes can be made up in bulk and frozen in meal-sized portions, to be served later warmed to blood temperature.

Cattery Casserole
We are grateful to Marion Kerr of Renfrewshire in Scotland for sending us this mouth-watering recipe, which she brought over from the Karori Cattery in Wellington, New Zealand. The tasty mixture of meat and vegetables will provide a well-balanced meal for the elderly cat, full of energy to beat the winter cold.

900g (2lb) tripe
450g (1lb) beef/chicken/turkey
225g (8oz) lamb's liver
225g (8oz) lamb's kidney
175g (6oz) organic brown rice
85g (3oz) pearl barley

175g (6oz) organic porridge oats
450g (1lb) mixed vegetables, fresh, frozen or tinned (use water-packed and include carrot, corn, asparagus, beans, peas, spinach, pumpkin, broad beans and celery) good sprinkle of garlic powder/granules
1 generous teaspoon low-salt savoury spread parsley

Mince all the meat well in a food processor or mincer. Place in saucepan and cover with water, add the garlic and bring to the boil. Add the brown rice and pearl barley, return to the boil, add the vegetables and simmer for half an hour. Add the savoury spread, porridge oats and parsley and simmer for half an hour, stirring often. Add more water if necessary but aim at a fairly stodgy stew. Divide into suitable containers and freeze when cooled.

Feline F-Plan
The following low-fat, high-fibre diet is ideal for any elderly cat showing signs of a bulging midriff.
225g (8oz) fresh liver (calf, pig or lamb's)
350g (12oz) skinned chicken
4 teaspoons wheat bran powder
1 teaspoon vegetable oil
175g (6oz) cooked rice
balanced mineral and vitamin supplement powder

Boil, or preferably microwave, fresh liver and skinned chicken until cooked then add the cooked rice, and mince together. Mix in vegetable oil and a daily ration of balanced mineral and vitamin supplement powder. Feed about 100g (4oz) daily.

6

Best Behaviour

Our increased knowledge of geriatric management, dietary requirements and veterinary medicine means that our cats are living much longer than they used to do. Now we have come to realise that not only do they need more physical care, but they also require more consideration from the psychological point of view. We have entered an era of greater understanding of older and geriatric human patients, and modern human geriatric care has become more concerned with maintaining mental capability and self-awareness and with helping to improve the ability to appreciate life to as high a level as the body will allow. The same is true for our cats but, while there are certainly changes in the central nervous system over time, there have been no definitive studies to determine where, when or how these happen in our pets.

According to Dr John Bradshaw at the University of Bristol, older cats may be slower to accept change or to learn how to deal with new challenges. But he also suggests that many cats between eleven and sixteen years of age are mentally more flexible than younger animals, for example at learning about changes in the location of food sources. Perhaps in the feline world, too, there is no substitute for experience. Locomotory skills and reactions to the vocal messages of other cats also seem to remain largely intact in older cats. However, they are less able to get used to new experiences, such as loud noises, and so may react each time they hear a noise rather than begin to ignore the sound as younger cats do when they realise that it does not mean danger.

As with people, cats vary greatly in the ageing process. Some cats are mentally on the decline as early as eight or nine years of age, while others are as fiercely independent and active at twenty as they were at two. In the Old Cat Survey conducted by Claire Bessant and behaviourist Peter Neville in conjunction with readers of *Cat World*, 22 per cent of cats between the ages of twelve and fourteen were reported by their owners as undergoing behavioural changes, in keeping with their perception of an 'older cat', and 12 per cent underwent such changes a little earlier, between the ages of ten and eleven. Dr John Bradshaw from the University of Bristol suggests that a cat is not usually said to be functionally old until at least its sixteenth year, though this figure will clearly vary in response to the nutritional status, living conditions and health of any individual animal. There is no predicting why, when or how long it might be before a cat can be described as 'old', but each and every one of them will let us know in their own way when a little extra care is needed.

Of course, there are many changes in the behaviour of older cats that we would regard as normal and predictable because they are similar to the changes that we and other mammals encounter as we grow older. Few of these changes should be regarded as at all problematic for owners as they involve a reduction in activity level and an increasing willingness on the part of the cat to relax. But, just as people change their habits in their advancing years, cats, too, alter their behaviour.

This can be manifested in a rather nervous, withdrawn character who seeks out quiet places and, well aware of its slowed reactions and reduced abilities to deal with disturbances or escape challenges, avoids positions or situations where it might fail. Such cats may become nervous recluses unless carefully maintained at some level within the social life of the household. And, while aggression problems are infrequent in cats anyway, and grow even less likely in old cats, some animals become spitty, recalcitrant and downright cussed in their old age. Should you disturb them when sleeping or eating or move them when they want to be left where they are, they can swear like a trooper or lash out with an aged, but still well-armed paw to keep control of their own destiny. However, for most, age brings relaxation and wisdom, a calmer and less ruffled attitude to life and a strengthening of their relationship with their owners.

HUNTING FOR OLD SPORTS

In the Old Cat Survey sample group, 163 of the total 180 cats enjoyed free access to the outdoors and could hunt if they wished. Asked whether their cats hunted less since they turned twelve, surprisingly it was reported that most cats had never enjoyed much success in that area anyway – perhaps this is the secret of their longevity!

'All he ever managed was a tea bag,' replied one woman, 'and that was in his prime.' So there hadn't been a lot of change to observe in the hunting habits of this 'typhoo typhoon' in his twilight years. However, many owners had noticed a substantial reduction in the level of successful hunting by their elderly cat, and most reported that their pets hardly bothered trying at all in their dotage. The oldsters, although they would still hunt, usually lowered their sights to the odd small bird or mouse and even reverted to the favourite kittenhood prey of spiders and moths. One old champion survivor called Scrapper, who had cauliflower ears from lifelong encounters with his rivals, continued his hunting activities even though he had lost all his teeth. However, he did go for slightly easier targets such as birds trapped in the greenhouse. Obviously wisdom does come with age. Champion mouser Towser, born in one of Scotland's oldest distilleries in Perthshire, caught an average of three mice a day, making the total on his twenty-second birthday over 25,000 mice.

However, most older cats, like us, take life easier in old age, as the senses dull and reactions slow down. As it becomes less and less successful first at finding and then at stalking mice and garden birds, the older cat is bound to give up a little. Then, as its body demands more rest, and the cat opts for a comfortable life indoors in the warm, real hunting is replaced with occasional hunting bursts directed toward moving targets such as soft toys or trailed wool. Of course, the pet cat has no need to hunt to feed it, and it is logical to assume that, as it gets older, it will decide not to bother.

NEW TRICKS

Looking at feral cats around the world, it seems that the older members of colonies, living around the hotels of tourist resorts as culturally diverse as Tunisia, Israel, Kenya and the Virgin Islands, adopt a much less active approach to survival than hunting or foraging from waste bins. Instead, they tend to sit closer to people than the younger begging cats and are more friendly. No doubt they hope that their more decrepit and vagabond appearance will tug at the heart-strings of the hotel guests. This tactic usually works and they, and tiny kittens, always seem to do very well – without all the active cadging, swift stealing and spitty competition that often goes on between the fit, young adults.

For a feral cat, old age creeps up much earlier than for the pampered pet, and the 'geriatric' ferals are probably no more than about five or six years old. Clearly life is much shorter for them, and age takes its toll much sooner away from the comforts of a human home. In the tourist hotels, the feral cat can live a little longer than its shy counterpart on industrial estates or in woodlands, but only due to its strategy of playing on its looks and not because it maintains its hunting abilities any better in an ageing body.

Although life sounds tough on the feral cat, it is that way in nature for all wild or feral animals. Our pet cats are lucky that we protect them from the harsh realities of mother nature and that their appointment with the feline grim reaper can be put off, sometimes to the extent of perhaps even trebling their normal life expectancy.

OLD GAMES

If the older cat continues to hunt, putting a bell on its collar may be more effective at warning the birds and mice than it is when used on a younger cat. The older cat may be less supple and thus less able to control its neck movements in order to stalk as quietly as the younger cat. Young cats can prevent the bell from ringing until the very last pounce. A bell may help the cat to hang up its claws a little earlier if you really find the garden carnage of the adult cat hard to live with. However, the important point is this: whether we owners actively encourage our cats to stop hunting, or they simply become less and less willing or able as they get older, we should try to compensate.

Our cats may be living longer as a result of our love and care, but we must also accept the responsibility for keeping them psychologically and physically fit. For the finely honed predator pet, this means exercising the same instincts, senses and behaviour as it would have done automatically for itself when hunting as a young cat. Fortunately, this is an easy task, and it simply involves continuing with the same type of play that we have always enjoyed with our pets and rejuvenating them with games that perhaps we abandoned when they grew out of kittenhood.

KEEPING FIT THROUGH PLAY

Games for older cats are essentially the same as those for kittens, in that they revolve around chasing moving targets – it is just that the targets may need to be a bit slower or larger, and you will need to take account of the cat's shorter concentration span and quickness to tire. So it's back out with the large soft and safe toys attached to string being dragged jerkily and enticingly around chair corners and up on to the sofa. Get out the cardboard boxes in which even the oldest of cats often still love to sit and attack the lid flaps. Revive the tents of newspaper through which the cat will run and slither and then grab to shreds with its back feet. However, you have to be especially careful with balls of string or wool because the strands may get caught between aged teeth or on brittle claws and cause nasty injury. Be especially sure that any soft toys are safe by making certain that plastic eyes or loose 'mouse' tails can not be chewed off to expose dangerous sharp points, and that they cannot be accidentally swallowed.

Ideally, play lots of supervised games where you can see the cat and make sure that it comes to no harm. Give it two or three play sessions a day to simulate periods of hunting activity, and you will keep it as alert and finely tuned as its body allows – even if the cat may never be quite sharp enough to be an effective hunter and killer of real live prey again. Remember to let the cat rest when it's had enough of its workouts. After all, cats patrol slowly around their territory for quite long periods but only hunt and stalk in short bursts, so you will not need too much play to keep them fit.

YOUNG AT HEART

Don't forget that there will be days, perhaps when the sun shines, and spring is in the air, when the older cat will amaze you at just how fit and active it continues to be when it chooses. The coiled spring that lurks ever deeper within can suddenly unwind and, with astonishing speed, even the oldest of crocks with failing eyesight can still pursue and pin down a wind-blown leaf on the lawn or swat successfully at a fly on the window. And while these bursts of energy may be less frequent as the cat ages, they remain proof in themselves that cats cannot help but respond to the right cues of movement and, what's more, will benefit enormously from them. The older cat may even embark on an occasional 'mad half hour' of charging around the furniture and up and down the stairs with all its energy-releasing and reflex-sharpening benefits - in fact, some people with older cats say they do this more often than they did in their middle years. The more effort we owners put into stimulating the cat through play, the more the cats themselves will continue to play on their own and stay fit and healthy in old age.

Some cats seem to prefer to watch others at play rather than to get involved themselves, like grandparents watching their grandchildren playing on the swings. On fine days, they might chance a sedentary swing themselves. Similarly, old cats may play gently with a ball or toy, but, for the most part, they simply enjoy being around playful youngsters and watching them hone their hunting and social skills with their owners or other animals. Interestingly, one survey respondent said that some of her old cats liked to be right in the thick of any noisy games or very active play between her other cats or children, though they never actually wanted to get directly involved themselves. As ever, specific behaviour depends on the nature and whims of the individual cat.

ON THE HOME PATCH

Younger cats, especially those embarking on territory building in the neighbourhood, often get into fights, and they are also frequently referred to behaviour clinics for refusing to share their den and their territory with the new cat or kitten that their owners have decided to try and introduce. While all these problems do arise very occasionally in older cats, for most, they are the long-forgotten concerns of youth. By the time a cat may be classed as 'older', it will usually be far less concerned about squabbling with others outside, it will have learned to take most changes at home in its stride and it will have decided on a policy of either liking or huffily tolerating, but probably not waging war against, any new cats that are introduced indoors. We shall look in greater depth at the older cat's relationships with other cats, inside the home and outdoors, in chapter 7.

BORN UNDER A WANDERING STAR

As they enter the later stages of old age, many cats choose not to wander far from home and trot back indoors if disturbed. Others seem to lose their sense of direction and wander off aimlessly or lose their orientation around the home, the core to their territory. Some cats seem almost to forget some of their ties to their home base. This can be manifested by forgetting to come indoors, taking up residence in the shed, greenhouse or next door's front room for the comfort of the moment and then apparently forgetting to come home for dinner.

Such errant cats will need to be let out at convenient times when the owner can watch their movements, perhaps supervise them in their own garden and see where they end up snoozing so that they can be brought in later for meals or for the night. It also helps to alert neighbours of the cat's ageing state of mind and to put a name and address on a collar identity tag, so that the cat can be returned home if found elsewhere. By the time this becomes necessary, it is extremely unlikely that the cat could suffer the risk of getting its collar caught on a branch, and it is also extremely unlikely to be stolen. The identity tag could, on the other hand, make all the difference to ensuring that the cat is brought home safely if it does wander too far away.

One owner of an old cat went as far as putting a note by the doorbell asking anyone returning their old cat from his lost wanderings to post him through the cat flap if they were out. Indeed, wandering away from the home patch is a quite likely behaviour in the senile cat and, while such itinerant activity can be supervised, most older cats will not wander too far before being picked up. However, if a cat really starts to get lost on a regular basis, it may be time to start to walk it on a harness and lead for outdoor exercise and fresh air, or confine it in a large outdoor pen in the garden on fine days. This will prevent large-scale wanders when the cat may only become distressed and confused and put itself at risk on unknown roads or from local dogs.

PRESERVING THE STATUS QUO

Older cats may also be less tolerant of changes to their territory. Yet, while new challenges outdoors may simply force them to seek out quieter and unchanging spots, the story indoors is different; here moving the furniture or redecorating can seriously disturb them. It is worth bearing this in mind if you have an older cat, and especially if you are planning to move home, or if the cat is a little hard of hearing or has failing eyesight and needs to rely on its sense of smell. Older cats may need much slower and more careful introductions to new homes and changed areas. Supervised introductions, one room at a time, over a period of weeks, with lots of love and affection and perhaps temporarily feeding them in each room with a litter tray handy as they explore will help them accept the changes.

GOOD GROOMING

Cats spend much of their day grooming themselves, especially on waking and after eating. Such attention to detail removes dirt, dander and parasites and spreads protective oils evenly over the coat for weatherproofing. Frequent licking with the specially rasping tongue helps to layer the hair and to streamline the coat for comfortable movement to enable quiet, stealthy hunting.

A SOCIAL FUNCTION

On hot days, evaporation of saliva from the coat helps keep the cat cool, but as it gets older and can rely on central heating or other forms of temperature control in the home, the older cat may find that it needs to groom less. Despite this, most still spend long, instinctive hours washing and grooming, and there is little doubt that much of this occurs in the pursuance of self-relaxation therapy. Friendly cats groom each other to seal and maintain social bonds, and cats will wash us and perhaps even lick our hair for the same reason, even if we restrict ourselves to stroking by hand and the odd kiss.

WITH A LITTLE HELP FROM MY FRIENDS ...

For most short-haired varieties, mother nature has provided the cat with the perfect grooming tools of tongue and forepaws and an enormously supple body to reach all those places, and owners rarely, if ever, need to get involved. Until old age that is. With stiffening of joints, reduced production of natural oils in the skin, falling concentration spans, longer periods of crumpled sleep, laziness and forgetfulness, many old cats start to take on a bedraggled, dry and scurfy or scruffy appearance, and their fur may not layer so well. This alone can cause the cat to look 'old' and, while careful attention to diet may help improve the coat, a little daily effort with the brush and comb can keep the older cat looking spick and span. See chapter 8 for more tips on grooming.

GROWING OLD DISGRACEFULLY

Odd behaviours in older cats have been coming increasingly to light in the past few years. This is probably because behaviour therapy services are now widely available, and more owners of pets of any age are encouraged by their vets to look for professional assistance and to seek help when problems crop up. We owners have changed, too. We have learned to understand the behaviour of our cats far more in recent times and have come to perceive greater value in the individual relationships we share with them. Increasingly, these relationships are based on respect, an attribute of all relationships that improves with the age of both owner and cat. Compared with, say, the all-too-ephemeral joys of owning a playful kitten, they are more deeply satisfying and enduring.

ON BEST BEHAVIOUR

In comparison with the young cat of six to eighteen months old, or even the adult up to the age of eight, old cats present very few behaviour problems indeed. The sagacity of age that old people usually acquire through a lifetime of experience applies perhaps even more to the older cat. It has learned how to behave in the human den, when to be part of the social scene and when not, how to let everyone know what it wants when it wants it and how to occupy the best spot for snoozing where it won't be disturbed or get in anyone's way. In fact, the older cat gets easier to look after as time goes on. Behaviour problems as such are far more likely to arise as signs of illness or of the body 'wearing out', or just through the cat's greater need for company and reassurance. Behaviour problems in young or adult cats stem from inabilities to learn about house-training, or recover from training breakdowns caused by nervousness or conflicts with other cats. They may spray urine, defecate openly or scratch marks on furniture and walls around the house. These are all signs that they are under social threat from the presence of other cats indoors or out or, most commonly, because they perceive their den to be under some unresolvable challenge as someone has moved the furniture, or had a friend or a dog to stay. Most upset can be caused when the security of the home has been destroyed by installing a cat flap in the door, so the cat's bed, food bowl and owner's lap are suddenly available to all its rivals.

SECURITY AT NIGHT

Without doubt, the most common behaviour problem in older cats is that of the nocturnal yeller. In the Old Cat Survey, of the 57 per cent of owners who reported that their cat had started to call out to them for attention and affection since it became an older member of the feline community, two-thirds did so at night. Owners had found themselves awoken in the night by plaintive cries from their pet. On the first occasion, they naturally leaped out of bed to see what had upset their much loved old cat – had it suddenly been struck by a crushing illness or the afflictions of age? When they find their cat, however, it is often just outside their bedroom door or pacing around downstairs by the door nearest to them, and it looks the picture of elderly health that it did at tea the night before.

PAINS OF SOLITUDE

Usually, owners find that their beloved pet is not in any physical distress at all and does not even seem to want anything in particular, such as to be fed or let out. To discover this, owners need to touch and examine their cat and ask it questions in a concerned and reassuring voice. All their cat wants is a little physical reassurance and protection in the lonely silence of the night, and then it quickly settles down happily after being 'tucked in' again. However, for the cat, two major events have occurred.

First, the ageing animal has conceded to itself that, after years of being independent and perhaps rather aloof, even shunning attention from its owners when it wanted solitude, the time has come when it values their presence. Through feeling lonely or a little insecure, the older cat has now accepted that some of that warm, human contact could make everything right. If it can get its owners to be present, then the cat can leave all vital decision-making to them for a while.

PAVLOVIAN SKILLS

The second major event to notice is that the clever cat has now trained its owners, in true Pavlovian style and with all the skill of a champion dog handler, to respond to its demands. It has realised that, with one pitiful cry, its owners will leap to its side at any time of day, but especially at night, to supply heaps of reassuring comfort. So, naturally, the next time the cat is feeling a little unsure of life, or simply doesn't feel like facing up to making a major decision – such as 'Shall I lie next to the radiator or in my favourite sun spot?' – it will utter the same cry. Now the clever cat is assured that its owners will come and help it to make up its mind by finding the most comfortable bed, or offering the better option of a good cuddle and then being put where it will be most content.

Age brings its own rewards for the cat, especially once it has learned how to use its voice to full effect, when it can no longer physically attract its owners' attention by either jumping on them or rubbing around their legs. As for the night-time problem, one respondent of the Old Cat Survey described at loving length how a cat basket had been placed next to her side of the bed to deal with any middle of the night requirements. However, many other owners, who perhaps might otherwise have suffered from the cries of the nocturnal old yeller, continue to enjoy peaceful nights of sleep – because their cat has been sleeping safe and quiet on their bed for years anyway.

REJUVENATING SLEEP

It is important to recognise that, like older people, older cats may change their sleeping habits. Both spend a greater proportion of their time asleep than in their youth, but the periods of sleep are likely to become either short and frequent, or very long and punctuated by quite long periods of being awake but in less of a routine. Thus an older person may lose the sleeping habits of a lifetime and spend much of the late morning and afternoon dozing or asleep, but they will then watch television long into the small hours of the night, go to bed very late, but wake early in the morning and be active.

NOT MOUSING BUT DOZING

Cats are rather different. In the wild they would be most active at dawn and dusk to coincide with the main foraging times of their rodent prey. As man's pet, the cat usually focuses time in the den around feeding times imposed by the owners and their availability to engage in social contact. As a result many cats naturally follow the activity patterns of their owners. They may sleep in past dawn, get up during daylight to be offered breakfast, indulge in a little late-morning hunting around the recently stocked bird-table and then lie up for the afternoon in a sun spot. They awake at the sound of the family arriving home from work and school and enjoy a little social contact before dinner is served and then catch the evening hunt before returning last thing to curl up asleep for the night.

This might be an average day for the average adult cat, which, like the 'average human', does not exist. In the Old Cat Survey, owners certainly reported that their cats spent more time sleeping, perhaps, as one loving owner said, 'Dreaming of the times when mice didn't run so fast.' Only 8 per cent spent less than 50 per cent of their time asleep, 58 per cent were estimated to spend 50 to 75 per cent of every 24 hours in the land of nod, and 29 per cent of our old cat sample, perhaps the oldest of all, was only awake for a quarter of the day or less.

LEARNING TO SAY NO

A cat's behaviour pattern varies according to the seasons, the weather, weekends and school holidays. It will also vary according to whether food is provided in distinct meals or, as is the case with many dry diets, permanently on offer for free-choice feeding. As the pet cat gets older, it will tend to sleep more at those times when it would have been out hunting and generally co-ordinate its time in the home with the presence of the owners. Even if it doesn't interact socially with them as much as it used to, the important thing is that they are there, providing security, and available for social contact if the older cat feels the need for some affection. The older the animal becomes, the more likely it is that it will look for them when disturbed or startled, or if it simply wakes up and finds itself alone, which, after all, is most likely to occur at night.

So, if your old cat suddenly becomes a nocturnal yeller and disturbs your sleep, it may be time to let it sleep in the bedroom and derive comfort from your immediate presence if it happens to wake in the night. But, if you don't want to do this, try to ignore the cries for a while. If you get up, remember that you are simply rewarding the cat's lack of confidence and ensuring that it can rely on you even when there's no real need. The longer the cries fail to pay off, the longer the cat will perhaps stay confident and independent, and you will get a decent night's sleep again.

COSY CORNERS

But, for most older sleep-a-lot cats, it is a case of ensuring that they have a warm, comfortable and draught-proof bed on which to doze away their lives, where they won't be disturbed by other younger and active cats, or the kids or the family dog (*see* tips on sleeping and comfort in chapter 8). Many cats develop a preference for sleeping in one particular place. Some sleep mainly on their owner's bed, both for comfort and the added security of being surrounded by their owner's scent, others select a soft armchair, and many choose a spot by a radiator or in the warm airing cupboard. One cat in the survey had opted to sleep on the toilet seat.

In terms of overall activity and sleep patterns, no two days are likely to be the same. Some days the older cat may seem to sleep through, especially during cold or wet weather, and not 'get up' at all, even to eat. This lethargy and apparent lack of appetite should not necessarily sound alarm bells unless accompanied by other signs, as it is highly likely that the next day, the cat will be up and about much more, eating a lot and sleeping less. The proportion of non-getting-up days to getting-up days will, however, usually become greater as the cat gets ever more ancient.

TOILET HABITS

Some old cats develop toilet problems around the house when they become very elderly. In the survey, only 30 older cats of the 180 respondents had begun to do so, though perhaps many more could be expected to develop problems in this area as they approach their final weeks or months of life. After all, if they have lived this long, the chances are that house-training has become a well-established tenet that will only be broken because of very understandable reasons, which will be mostly medical in origin. Owners of old and incontinent cats are usually resigned to coping with clearing up in good spirit, and one owner commented, 'He's not so much of a pleasure nowadays because of his inappropriate toilet habits, but now he's an old man and has given us great pleasure throughout his life, he deserves our tolerance' – a sentiment and attitude often expressed by our survey respondents.

As we know, human geriatrics quite often become incontinent to varying degrees because the sphincters (the muscles that close openings, such as the bowel) start to loosen with age, and the hormone systems that control such bodily functions as bladder-filling time become less precise. Most cats are most meticulous in their toilet habits and teach themselves as tiny kittens to use rakeable, movable material, such as cat litter indoors, or garden soil outdoors, when nature calls. Problems usually only occur in the adult cat if it gets shut in and cannot get out or is denied access to its litter tray. There are many other reasons for a breakdown in house-training in the fit adult cat, but these are none the less rare and can often be treated successfully with appropriate behaviour therapy, leaning on the cat's natural instinct to keep its living, eating and sleeping areas clean.

SECURITY PROBLEMS

Some breakdowns in house-training in cats young and old, however, are caused by security problems. A typical example would be where the owners have installed a cat flap to allow their cat easy access, but, in so doing, they may also have allowed all their cat's rivals to enter its den. This alone can be enough to set the cat urinating and defecating indoors so as to leave chemical signals around the place, which reinforce its own feelings of security by pervading the atmosphere with its own smell and perhaps identifying its occupancy to the intruders. In some cases, urine will be sprayed against such vertical marking posts as chair legs and door frames, while, in others, the stressed cat will simply leave a large puddle or a messy pile on an armchair, bed or mat.

If the intruder cats also eat your cat's food, lie in its bed or leave their own calling cards around the place, this is even more likely to be upsetting. In the case of older cats, it is worth bearing in mind that, while they may have been happily using a cat flap for years and still keep their rivals at bay, with age, they may become less and less able to do so. Aware of their failing competence, they may then resort to urinating, spraying or defecating in a desperate effort to keep up appearances.

In such cases, it is clearly time to offer a little more protection and board up the cat flap. If the cat needs to be popping outside to relieve itself a little more often than it used to, closing its door to the world may equally cause house-training problems – it's the same stuff but deposited for a different reason! In these cases, a selective cat flap where the cat wears a magnetic or electronic 'key' on its collar, which only releases the flap catch at its approach, may keep the den secure but still enable the cat to pop out when nature calls. It should go without saying that scolding, smacking a cat or, most heinous of all, 'rubbing its nose in it' will only make the problem worse. Such reactions will make the cat feel even less secure in its home and will have no reformative effects on the deposition of urine or faeces around the home – whatever the original reason for the cat's behaviour.

CAUGHT SHORT

One of the first signs of senility cited by owners of old cats is a loss of toilet control, but, aside from medical complications, such as cystitis, which may also be prevalent in old age, problems usually occur only in the most frail and ancient of old cats. Nevertheless, before this happens, many other more mature cats may develop house-training problems because of a growing reluctance to go outdoors. After all, if you have decided to hang up your weapons and no longer go out to hunt, the chances are that you will lose the habit of braving the rain or cold to pop out for a pee and look for alternative and warmer facilities indoors.

An odd accident may be acceptable to owners on bitter winter days, but many more cats convince their owners all too easily that they simply cannot go outdoors any more. For some, this reluctance has sad and terminal repercussions as less tolerant owners may then presume that their cat is becoming senile because of the incontinence and have it put to sleep. But, when odd accidents become frequent puddles or smelly deposits in specific sheltered areas, such as behind an armchair, on the doormat or in the wardrobe, it is time to assess just how old the cat really is.

INDOOR LOOS

For the healthy older cat, a little encouragement and the re-establishment of a routine of being put out may be all that is needed to ensure that it is in the right place at the right time to resolve such problems. But, if the cat is genuinely finding life a bit tough on the outside and shows other physical signs of age, such as stiffness of the body and the need to pass urine frequently, it may be time to pay attention to its toilet requirements indoors again, even if you have had many litter-tray-free years. The simple provision of a tray or two, perhaps on the site that the cat has chosen to soil, may provide it with a suitable facility and bring a happy halt to the 'inconvenience'.

Alternatively, providing trays where the cat has easy access to them, near a favourite sleeping spot for example, can help ensure that it can get to a loo when it is most likely to need to go, such as immediately on waking. It may be helpful to have several trays around the house if the cat is used to having free access. A tray in the kitchen should be provided for use after eating, but not sited too close to food because this in itself is the cause of many breakdowns in house-training. Cats don't want to go to the toilet too close to where they eat, any more than we would want to eat in the loo. If the older cat is usually played with or particularly active in a given room, a tray there will also help it to get things in the right place, especially after periods of activity when it is also most likely to need to use the toilet.

CAT FLAPS

While cat flaps can be the cause of many house-training and indoor marking problems, old cats could benefit from the installation of one if there are no local rival cats, or it is on friendly terms with them anyway. However, while a flap may allow easy access to the outdoors, when the older cat gets caught short, many may find difficulty in learning to use it if they have never known one. They may also lack the physical strength or balance to push the flap open, so it is always worth propping it open with a length of wood or plastic or tying it open with string, when you want the cat to go out, and then locking it shut and offering litter trays nearby as alternatives for the desperate cat, when you don't.

The older cat should not be expected to have to climb up too high to get through the flap, nor face a long drop on the other side, a point to remember when installing the flap. If its position is already making entry and departure difficult for the old cat and perhaps exacerbating house-training problems, providing a small ramp on one or both sides of the flap can make life more convenient.

COVERED TRAYS

Some older cats, used to having a tray in the house, may develop a bad aim in their final months and years. They get themselves to the tray as accurately as ever, and they manage to get in it all right and dig a wee hole. But then they squat with their bottoms hanging over the side and pee on the floor next to the tray. While this may keep the litter fresh for much longer than usual, it is clear that the cat needs a little help at this stage. A covered tray, either of a proprietary brand or homemade with an inverted cardboard box with a cat-flap sized hole cut in the end or the simple provision of plastic boards down three sides of the tray, will usually ensure that the cat gets into the right position and will keep its aim accurate.

Covered trays are probably better for the cat that has not been used to a tray indoors. These provide all round and overhead security at that most vulnerable of moments, when the cat is likely to have closer company than it has been used to. Many of the modern designs include an odour-filter in the roof to help keep the home smelling fresh. Positioning of the litter tray is crucial if the older cat is to feel confident about using it. As well as being placed well away from feeding dishes and drinking bowls, the tray should also be far from known conflict areas, such as the dog's bed, and not in main thoroughfares of the house or particularly active areas, such as where children play.

ALLOWING FOR ACCIDENTS

But, despite the best of management plans, it is almost inevitable that there will be a few accidents with the older cat. It is important, therefore, that, having been caught short, the cat does not then come to think of the area as its latrine and keep returning to the same place. Effective cleaning is essential and, despite the excess of proprietary solutions available, there is little to beat a scrub with a warm solution of a strong biological washing detergent, a rinse with cold water and gentle agitation with an alcohol, such as ethanol, surgical spirit or even vodka!

Always check first that this system does not remove the dye from loved carpets by testing a hidden corner. Afterwards, leave all treated areas to dry completely, perhaps even to the point of using a hair drier on the damp spots, before allowing the cat back to sniff and explore. The cleaning should have removed all traces of the smell of the cat's urine or faeces, and this is crucial in ensuring that the animal is not attracted back to the same spot.

The importance of the area to the cat can also be altered by feeding some of its daily ration at the now clean, dry place, so that it becomes seen as a zone in its den where it wouldn't want to go to the toilet, in the same way as feeding close to the litter tray in the kitchen may deter it from using it there. If this is inconvenient, a small saucer with dry cat food stuck to it can act as a deterrent, without making a mess and without becoming depleted and losing its effect if the cat tries to eat the food.

CONTAINMENT

If, despite all these provisions and treatment, accidents become more frequent, it may be time to check the type of litter on offer. Pellet litters, in particular, may be uncomfortable for an older cat to stand on if the pads of his paws have softened through a life indoors on the carpet. Fine-grain litters, either of the commercial variety or in the form of sand, will often prove more appropriate and encourage the older cat to keep using its trays.

It is important to keep an eye on the contents of dirty litter trays when cleaning them out, as an increase in the frequency of urination may indicate a medical problem, such as failing kidneys, which needs urgent veterinary attention. A lack of faeces, on the other hand, may indicate constipation and, again, the sooner the cat is examined by the vet the more likely it is that treatment will be successful for the older cat. This is especially important when a lack of continence becomes the norm in a senile cat. Some older cats will help with this examination because, though they continue to use their trays, they may forget to cover up after themselves.

There are drugs that have been used in dogs to increase the blood supply to the brain and improve alertness in geriatric patients, though, as yet, these are not licensed for use with elderly cats. When, despite the best of care and management changes, toilet problems show no signs of containment, owners are best advised to restrict the movements of the cat to a small area to minimise the impact of its incontinence on home hygiene. This in itself can help maintain the cats aim for a while longer and is a commonly used technique for treating breakdowns in house-training in younger, fitter cats.

But, if the older cat becomes upset at this necessary restriction and continues to soil its smaller living area or has great difficulty in keeping itself clean around the rear end, even with assistance, it is usually fair to assume that its quality of life has diminished to such an extent that euthanasia maybe the kindest alternative (*see* chapter 9). Similarly, once a cat starts to urinate or defecate wherever it happens to be or to soil its sleeping area, voluntarily or involuntarily, and then lie in it, it may be time to take the most caring, but most difficult, decision of all. But by working through a programme of containment, a cat's life may have been prolonged by several weeks or months when perhaps, in times past, it might have been taken on its final trip to the vet for just a couple of messy accidents.

STAYING CONTENT AND VIGILANT

Without doubt, the way to avoid the problems of senility in the old cat and not only prolong its life but also increase its quality of life is to invest time and care as soon as any signs of debilitation, medical or psychological, are noticed. Being aware that the older cat may be upset by changes to the home, social disruptions or medical conditions, we can help make life easier for it and protect it from any possible long-term trauma, about which, when it was younger, no one would have needed to worry.

Cats are, after all, not obligatory social animals like dogs. They are friendly and sociable with human beings and usually some other cats because of the pleasure it brings them. In old age, possibly for the the first time since they were kittens with their mother many years earlier, they may have to depend on another for their security, health, protection and stimulation, and they may come to need social relationships again.

This realisation can come as a shock to some cats, but if we take the same positive attitude as we ought to adopt with our own parents as they grow old – one that takes account of failing abilities but that motivates and stimulates within the capabilities of the old body – our old cats will continue to enjoy their time on earth. And, as a vital incentive to keep on trying with them, we can discover new and rewarding depths to our relationship with our cats – even as they age.

7

Old Friends

Older cats seem to be more affectionate than younger felines and enjoy the company of both family and friends, seeing them as an infinite source of love and attention. Most of us want to fuss over our cats and have a loving cuddle, and as the oldies love fuss and attention and seem to revel in feeling special the pleasure is mutual. Younger cats are not so amenable as they can get over excited, and the embrace often ends in a grabbed and chewed hand, or they may simply get bored and run off in search of more exciting happenings.

This mutual affection makes many ageing moggies realise that they have secured a venerable position in the household, and they perpetuate this with their amazing sense of dignity. All of this ensures that their commands at home are never taken lightly, and that the giver or respondent feels good at seeing to their every whim – a very clever ploy. Mix affection and dignity with the odd eccentricity, and you have a strong and lovable character always ready for a friendly chat or willing to listen to your tales of woe on a bad day and purr away your depression.

WILL YOU STILL NEED ME?

Many old cats take liberties, such as eating at the table with everyone else, getting into their owner's bed and waking them up at 5 a.m. for a snack or to refill the hot-water bottle that has gone cold. They would never have got away with all this in kittenhood but over time have cleverly wheedled such behaviour into their repertoire, One cat owner succumbed to the wiles of her treasured puss to the extent that: 'He sleeps in the bed beside me, and I just wrap my arms around him and turn him over when I shift. He puts his head on the pillow and goes to sleep for the night.' Years of getting used to each other's sleeping rhythms have enabled cat and woman to relax together almost better than husband and wife. Another cat lover, resigned to the shift in power relations with an ageing pet, added that their cat selected a different person in the household each morning and then would only pester him or her for what she wanted that day – you could argue that she was being very democratic in her choice of 'slave for the day'. As one woman in the survey put it, 'One of the advantages of having an older cat is the rapport that has built up over the years – after all, it can take quite a while to train a human.'

WILL YOU STILL FEED ME?

Apart from the dubious honours of serfdom bestowed upon the owners of older cats, there are other more certain advantages. Older cats have the benefit of ease of management if, for example, you are out at work all day. They are happy to rest indoors rather than risk all the dangers of the outdoors. They don't get bored or lonely when left on their own, preferring to sleep away the hours in a warm spot. Gone are the days of coming home to find curtains pulled down on to the floor by crazy kitten frolics, chewed jumpers, broken vases and toys unburdened of their stuffing.

WHEN I'M 64

As considered 'adult' friendship and respect for our pet cat replaces the admiration of its youthful reflexes, this is, in turn, superseded by a calmer, relaxed era of company for its own sake with the ageing predator. It is not hard to see why we owners love our old cats with such intensity. After all, the cat may have been part of the family and stayed at home for long after the kids have finished school, packed their bags and left home. Our now ageing cat may have seen the passing of nappies, their first day at school, the first boy or girlfriend, the first job and the fleeing from the nest, and now it settles back with what is left of the kids' parents to enjoy its last few months or years in relative peace.

All of this can complete the circle of life for mum and dad and enable them to maintain their parental nurturing instincts by looking after their old puss, taking them back perhaps to the time when only the three of them shared the family home. If all this sounds a little too rosy and contrived, the inescapable fact is that the sedate attitude to life of the old cat can impart and reflect a similar atmosphere at home. And in a world that we owners contrive to make increasingly stressful for ourselves with our work, social and sporting commitments, the old cat can be just the tonic to ensure that we unwind when we do get home. As one owner commented, 'Misty is relaxation personified' – which can only have positive repercussions on the quality of life.

LAID-BACK LIFE

Most owners in the Old Cat Survey suggested that their cats were more laid-back in their later years, enjoying attention and interacting more with the family and visitors than when they had territorial and hunting business to attend to out of doors. Many owners spent long years coaxing what had been stray or rescued cats, often from unfortunate domestic backgrounds, to participate in family life. Over the years, a lot of cats had indeed become well socialised and grown into affectionate trusting pets, giving their owners immense pleasure – yet old age wasn't necessarily something that they had noticed in their cats, any more than they had noticed any sudden changes in themselves. Indeed, the survey's questionnaire, with twelve as the cut-off age that defined the cat as 'elderly', forced many owners to notice just how long their cat had been with them.

Few owners in the survey said that they missed the kittenish antics of their cats. Destroying knitted garments, fridge-raiding, overturning potted plants, climbing the curtains and springing from nowhere to grab people's legs may have been fun and delightful at the time, but, on reflection, all of this had been replaced by a deeper and different friendship. Recognition of age and its incumbent limitations on activity and behaviour is a traditional subject for lamentation by us humans, and for many it is accompanied by a concerted effort to look and keep as physically young as possible. But cats appear to take their passing years without such regrets, and most are models of peaceful acceptance and adaptation of activity, ensuring that their lifestyles remain as pleasurable as possible.

As the years pass by slowly and contentedly, the cat is very likely to adjust the nature of its relationships with its owners, their friends and visitors, and the other cats and pets with which it shares its den. Most such adjustments are less concerned with keeping up appearances or trying desperately to give the impression of maintaining competence to deal with any challenge, and more with taking life as it comes, steadily expecting more of others as and when required – from the owners at least!

With very few exceptions, we are more than happy to provide whatever the cat wants and perhaps put up with the few downsides of increased veterinary bills, because the old cat deserves such attention and its demands seem so much less. The old cat also shows an increased willingness to be near us when it is feeling sociable, and this in turn adds to our nurturing feelings for it and ensures that we feel more protective and sociable towards our pet. One owner summed it up succinctly, 'Our cat is more pleasure these days – she feels secure in our love of her now.'

CAT CALLS

In the Old Cat Survey, 64 per cent of owners said that generally their cats demanded more attention, while 57 per cent said that their cats had begun to call out to them when they wanted attention or affection. In some cases this increased dependency caused a problem, as we also saw in chapter 6: 'Like old people, he wakes early at around 5 a.m. If I don't get up, he goes downstairs and really cries until I give him attention,' said one sufferer. But, for many owners, their older cat's demands could be more readily accommodated with a little organisation.

QUALITY TIME

'My older moggies have their own particular times of day when I give them undivided attention – on my knee for breakfast in the morning, and again in the evening when I am watching television.' This is ideal for the older cat, which will usually prefer longer periods of undisturbed petting and stroking to the frequent short encounters that suited its more active lifestyle when it was younger. In other words, the older cat may start to seek out its owners for longer periods of attention when they are most settled, relaxed and still. 'Old cats like a fuss made of them and to be made to feel special' – and why not? When you're old, you deserve it, and it seems that few owners are unwilling to supply affection on demand.

As time goes by, old cats can be expected to become increasingly demanding of their owners. Some follow them around the house and garden to satisfy their needs for physical protection and emotional security. 'He even follows me down the road if I'm not careful to shut him in when I go out,' remarked one owner who, despite such inconvenience, clearly enjoyed her cat's increased need for her and wasn't worried that it might be becoming something of a social inadequate after a life of fierce independence.

FINDING A VOICE

'He's become much more emotionally dependent on me and my family since he reached fourteen and calls loudly if he doesn't know which room I'm in.' Many owners report that their older cats are much more vocal and learn to use their voices to make their demands felt. Many ask to be let out or petted, as well, for specific demands of attention at night. They may extend their requirements to enable them to do all sorts of things, such as being helped down on to the floor from high places, from where it would be uncomfortable to jump unaided. It seems that, once a cat has learned to use its voice in a social context and especially to manipulate its owners, a whole new world of social intercourse opens up to it: 'She has always been pleasantly talkative, but nowadays she has an opinion about everything!' said one.

LEARNED HELPLESSNESS

While it can be flattering to be loved and wanted, many owners are also a little suspicious of the true nature of their cat's dependency, and some suspect that they are being conned: 'I taught him to ask to be lifted down from the windowsill, now he expects it from the lowest footstool!' This type of unnecessary demand fits the description of 'learned helplessness' rather well. Many of our pets convince us that through some illness or inadequacy they can not cope with an aspect of their lives. Because this works when they are sick or injured, for example, they then continue to show similar signs, even when they have recovered their health and can cope perfectly well. A typical case of this, which behaviourists and veterinarians encounter, would be the 'psychogenic limp', practised by many a socially manipulative dog as an attention-seeking ruse when they feel that their owners are ignoring them. While cats in their prime are independent and have far less need than a dog in a pack of such social propping-up, in old age it seems that they can grow manipulative and easily convince us to spring to their attention.

One survey respondent wryly recorded how her cat, 'Seems to have forgotten how to use the cat flap, so he sits and waits for it to be pushed open, or the door to be opened for him.' And then, naturally enough for many cats, let alone an older one, he probably didn't always want to go out anyway. He was just proving the point that his owners would respond if he wanted them to – and they did.

Annoying as this behaviour may be, it does make us feel that we are more caring owners because we have recognised the cat's desire for something. However, from there it is just a short step to the commonly encountered older feline character that expects me to go to her, not her to come to me'.

POWER POLITICS

There is a balance of power in feline/human relationships of which the older cat is invariably aware as much as its owners. If it cries out unusually, then we owners respond because we are concerned that the cat may be in pain or feeling unwell. If our cat does become sick and require lots of TLC, it will be depending on us – perhaps needing to be hand-fed on specially prepared and warmed, easily digested food or requiring its brow mopped in case it gets too hot in front of the radiator, which the vet has advised us to put nearby to keep it warm. And when the animal recovers to full health, we shall be delighted, naturally, but perhaps be unaware that it has already been back on its feet for a while. Meantime, our creaky old cat has learned to love that all enveloping care. What is more, it now realises that the slightest show of weakness or incapacity on its part will make us stand to attention again.

There are younger cats and dogs aplenty that learn the same tricks but, with the added advantage of our fears about its age very much in its favour, the older cat is a master of manipulation. Old dogs just look helpless and derive attention that way, while their feline counterparts somehow make a monkey out of us – they convince us every time that they are actually going to die if we don't leap to their aid. On the one hand, we need to give lots of extra care to our unwell, older cat and accept, especially, that it will need more looking after than when it was young, partly because of the potential for greater emotional trauma. On the other, we need to guard against inadvertently teaching the cat to become overdependent on us or to manipulate us for extra attention well before it genuinely is needed.

The commonsense approach is to decrease the level of attention gradually as the cat recovers from illness and to err on the side of 'leaving them to it' as it comes to fend for itself again. However, in practice, it is almost impossible to predict how much leeway to give. Somehow, the cat will always remain in control of the situation. The word 'wily' always springs to mind as an apt description of the recovering and malingering older cat.

FELINE STRATEGIES

At night, as we saw in chapter 6, a spell of illness can constitute the first opportunity for an old cat to learn 'how to train your family' and is a prime example of how it can dictate its owner's behaviour at will. Some retain a sense of reasonableness about their demands, and they reserve a certain type of vocal request for help required in moments of genuine distress. When he's cold or hungry, he uses a special call (not a cry) for attention, said the owner of one decent, old cat.

However, many older cats are like young children: they enjoy attention and are clever enough to employ various strategies to get it. Like the toddler who pretends not to be hungry and has to be tempted with all sorts of treats to make it eat, old cats may similarly torture their concerned owners, who feel the old puss should have a good square meal to keep up its strength. They meow for attention and presumably food, but then they ignore what is put before them.

One woman reported, 'My old cat is a great pleasure to me, and life is very content except for my apparent inability to dish up the right food. He is extremely spoiled and what pleases him one day probably won't again for at least another month.'

Another remarked, 'He has recently started to demand more food and expects extra to be added or the bowl to be refilled each time he inspects it. He then only eats it if I am beside him.' While it is true that older cats probably want to eat smaller portions more often, they use the interactive feeding time as an excellent opportunity to make sure that owners are kept on their toes and on call.

Hand-feeding can become the norm, or the cat simply will not eat. This is doubtless because of the security and protection that being fed by hand can offer the cat; it helps it to relax and worry less about being challenged by other cats over a valuable resource. But then why not? Most cat owners want to nurture their pet and reciprocate their cat's need for them just as much. After all, everyone wants to be loved and needed, and experienced old cats instinctively know far more about rewarding our good behaviour – that is giving them what they want – than a whole class of students studying the psychology of learning.

MUTUAL UNDERSTANDING

Despite failing senses and physical limitations, it is clear that many older cats remain psychologically as bright as buttons and are certainly not one breath short of a purr when it comes to relating to their owners' behaviour. The ever-friendly cat often seems to become more aware of its owners' emotional state and as it grows older increasingly responds to their moods. This observation is open to some criticism, and owners are often very good at dismissing such suggestions as their cat's desire simply to sit on them for warmth and comfort. This interpretation may also result from owners' unacknowledged needs to relate to another being when feeling low – the older cat is more likely to be there in its usual place and is very willing to be talked to.

THE COMFORT OF CATS

But many cats, young and old, do spend hours and days beyond the call of duty keeping us company when we are lying in our sick beds, and the urge to help and comfort goes well beyond taking advantage of a warm bed and a receptive owner, or so we would like to believe. It is not unreasonable that an animal that now chooses to spend more time indoors and interact with us increasingly when it is awake should become more sensitive to our moods. Furthermore, it may seek to maintain its own security by looking for physical contact if we should show emotional, as well as physical, signs of upset. 'When I am sad, worried or unwell, he seeks me out and purrs loudly to me,' said one owner. What she did not mention was whether her cat had always done this, or whether it was a previously undiscovered and caring side to its character, which had only became apparent when the cat became older and grew to appreciate the joys of human contact and togetherness.

Increased mutual understanding is bound to occur if owner and older cat spend more time together than when they both pursued more activities away from home. As with other things in life, the more you put in, the more you get out: 'He has become more autocratic but more loving indoors ... we understand him perfectly,' was a quote that expressed the two sides of many older cats accurately as benevolent despots. Perhaps our animals do become more insistent on orderly rules for daily life. They do like to be left alone more to sleep and doze undisturbed, but they repay the effort they force us to make with increased affection and contact of a more considered nature, when awake and wanting to give it. The comparison with ourselves as we age is impossible to resist. 'Older cats are like OAPs,' said one woman, 'their moods change and they sulk if they don't get their own way.'

SWITCHING SENSES, NEW PRIORITIES

Older cats are certainly like older people in that they are often less tolerant of change to their home environment or routine than when they were young. This is especially true if they are becoming forgetful or losing their eyesight or hearing and cannot so readily assimilate or reconcile those changes into their daily life. Compensating for the physical effects of ageing is something that we humans find difficult, but cats often employ other senses or behaviour patterns.

It is difficult to appreciate just how much a cat takes in visually and aurally and that what for us can be the most thoroughly depressing sides of old age – the loss of sight and hearing – may be, to the cat, far less traumatic. As the effects of failing eyesight and deafness take hold, an older cat usually switches to using its sense of smell and touch through its whiskers, as we shall see later in chapter 8. In addition, once contact with a friend or owner is established, many an old cat will slip into overdrive with physical displays of arched back and furious rubbing against the outstretched hand to communicate. Such enhanced actions convince us all the more that 'he has become an affectionate old boy since his senses started failing him.'

The need to maintain vocal contact becomes ever more vital, as one might expect. Patience is required to put up with the yells and to remember to keep on responding: 'He uses a shrill, low meow, which drives me mad at times,' complained one old cat owner in our survey. This brings to mind a good description of how best to handle our old cats and that is: patiently. With a little patience, we can continue to enjoy each other to the full.

For sure, it is a nuisance when the old boy's teeth get loose and fall out as his gums recede, he may dribble uncontrollably all over us when we pet him. Yet, he probably always did salivate at such times when reminded of his first experience of close and affectionate social contact with his mother. Kittens are likely to be fed when they snuggle up to their parent, so, as cats relax with us 'mothers', they salivate because they associate the feeling with being fed. Now, however, there are fewer teeth and less gum to keep it all in. All you need, however, is the tolerance to get a flannel or towel and keep on stroking.

SOCIAL BUTTERFLIES

Many cats go further than being happier around their owners in their old age, and they will actively seek out visitors and house-guests for affection and social contact as well. When young, many will have shied away from visitors only to enjoy them in later life. Some are very active in pursuing their new social careers and pester visitors for attention. This can come as a great surprise to owners of cats who had spent years watching their pets avoiding their guests by darting out through the cat flap as soon as the doorbell rang.

Many cats do become generally more tolerant of visitors, including children, perhaps as a result of becoming more confident about their ability to avoid conflict or control unwanted attention with a good hiss and a swipe of the paw. On the other hand, perhaps their behaviour change has nothing to do with overcoming lifelong fears at all – for many, it may be just good old-fashioned bone-idleness.

Some old cats, however, do become more timid of visitors, especially with loud and unpredictable children, and may need a safe place to hide when strangers call. It may be kinder to put the cat in a quiet room with food and a litter tray when young relatives arrive.

SPECIAL RELATIONSHIPS

After years of living with a cat, most owners would say that their relationship grew special, but a few emerge as extra special, and perhaps the story that follows highlights the closeness between cats and owners, and the strength they can gain from one another.

It is a tale from Ann Haughie, a woman who runs a cattery and has done a great deal of work with feral cats. It was published in the *Feline Advisory Bureau Journal* in 1992:

For many elderly people living alone, their much loved pet may be their only friend. When old age is combined with a severe handicap, the animal may also provide a vital lifeline. This was the case with Evelyn and her 10-year-old, neutered male cat, Sandy.

When Evelyn, a profoundly deaf, insulin-dependent diabetic, was admitted to hospital in a coma following a fall, there were no friends or relatives to care for her cat, and I was approached by the hospital social worker for help. Sandy was also much distressed by his separation from Evelyn. He spent his time cowering in a corner of my cattery, lashing out at me whenever I approached. Evelyn was unconscious for several days, and it seemed she might not recover. The ward sister, a cat lover, suggested that a visit from Sandy might help. My initial protest that Sandy had fleas and what about the hospital rules, which demanded 'no animals on hospital premises', met with the response that Evelyn would be well used to Sandy's fleas, and some rules were made to be broken. I had already seen Evelyn attached to her life-support machine and did not hold out much hope for success, but I agreed to bring Sandy to Evelyn's room.

Several nurses and t he social worker gathered round the bed. I did not know how Sandy would react, given his behaviour towards me at home, but he did not protest as I lifted him out of the carrying box. Sister took Sandy and placed him in Evelyn's arms, telling her that Sandy had come to see her. Sandy was quite relaxed and reached out with his paw and patted the tube in Evelyn's nose. There wasn't a dry eye in the room when Evelyn's eyes eventually opened, and she recognised Sandy. The tube was temporarily removed to allow Sandy to snuggle close to Evelyn.

Evelyn remained in hospital for several weeks, and Sandy and I visited daily. Some days, Evelyn was barely conscious, and on others she was fractious, but Sandy would just sit quietly on her bed or in her arms. He seemed content to be near her, whatever her mood. He sat perfectly still when nurses came to change her catheter or to give injections. A smile would light up Evelyn's face whenever she realised that Sandy was there. When Evelyn was well enough to be moved into the main ward, arrangements were made for us to use a day-room so that Evelyn could enjoy her visit without upsetting patients who did not like cats or who might be allergic to them (this was a medical ward where some of the patients had chest infections).

Everyone looked forward to Sandy's visits. There was a constant stream of patients wanting to stroke Sandy or talk about their own much loved pet at home. I bought Sandy a harness to minimise the *risk of losing him through an open door. Evelyn, who has essentially lived in a world of isolation and silence, became quite a chatterbox and demonstrated that she was a skilled lip reader, if only people would give her a chance of conversation. During these sessions it occurred to me that the hospital had special rooms set aside for smokers whose anti-social habits are a known health hazard, so why not a special room where patients could be visited by their beloved animal friends whose presence might alleviate much anxiety and stress?*

Evelyn's illness has since necessitated hospital admission on several occasions. Each time Sandy has been welcomed as her friend whose presence is essential to recovery. She is no longer able to care for herself at home but, after much discussion with the local authority, the inhuman. 'No pets in council accommodation' rule was relaxed to allow Evelyn to take up residence in sheltered accommodation together with Sandy, where they can continue to give each other the love and support that gives their life meaning.

Few cat owners will have a dry eye after reading this. It so clearly illustrates the strength of the bond between woman – one who could be so easily ignored or rejected by her own species – and cat and their mutual support for one another.

TOP CATS

INDOORS

In the Old Cat Survey, owners were asked about their older cats' attitude towards other cats. Some 20 per cent were reported as seeking out the companionship of cats, 46 per cent avoided other cats and 34 per cent showed aggression towards other cats. The behaviour of 37 per cent of cats had changed as the cat aged. Two of the cats played together more than they had when they were younger, enjoying a return to kittenhood. But age does not always affect the social behaviour of the older cat; many show no behavioural changes in relation to other cats, and some still prefer the company of dogs. Of course, much depends on whether the old cat is expected to share its home base with other cats, and what its history has been of sociability indoors. This will usually be rather distinct from its behaviour towards other cats outdoors.

The cat that walks by itself?

Many cats become more sociable, or at least more tolerant if they are left alone and allowed to move around when and where they want. 'He's mellowed and become more tolerant of other cats in the house' is what one might hope for with an older cat among many younger cats – especially if you have had a life as peace-maker between warring cats in the home. We might even wish for the effects of age to occur sooner in some pugilistic cats. 'He's changed from being a fighter to a spectator,' said another owner, something that would make life much easier for a lot of multi-cat households.

Equally one might feel sorry for the demotion in rank and self-esteem that may accompany the ageing process in some cats. The comment 'He's less assertive – he used to be top cat' implies some degree of sympathy for an old deposed controller. Some maintain their power in the den despite advancing years: 'Paddington is still boss cat – no other cat can usurp him.' Yet this, surely, was only a question of time, and perhaps Paddington is one of those very fit older cats who will need physical decline, rather than an active choice, to forgo his urge to control and rule those around him.

Power shifts

If you own several cats, there may be a shift in power as an older one takes a step down and becomes generally less competitive over status or resources. Provided it has access to a warm place to rest, where it may dig in its paws and insist on its rights, it will be content there. The other cats, having cordoned it off socially to the one area, will then leave it alone and take over the rest of the den. However, if the older one is forced down rather than abdicating, there may be aggressive confrontations. These may lead to upset, associated soiling and indoor marking and a general instability for some time until things calm down.

Occasionally an older or ill cat may be bullied by others keen to seize the opportunity of exploiting its weakness. 'She used to be boss but now two other cats have climbed the ladder and boss her,' remarked one owner. Another wrote to say, 'When her own mother was terminally ill, she spat at her.' Though this may sound like an ungrateful child taking unfair advantage of the frailties of age, it is more likely due to the changing smells of the skin oils or pheromones in the urine of the mother. These changes would be caused by the disease itself or the effects of any medication on her scent profile, causing recognition breakdowns, rather than by a shift in the real and underlying social relationship. Loss of familiarity breeds contempt in such cases, and we can all too easily forget just how much social familiarity between cats depends on scent recognition, even between such long-established and continuous relationships as a daughter and her mother.

Finally, in houses with several crumbly cats, sometimes indolence rules OK. Relations between individuals can tend to improve simply because the ageing felines can no longer be bothered to get up and do anything about it. They may just stick to their own 'space', into which it is clear that others may not intrude.

BRINGING IN NEW CATS

Most old cats may be less inclined to fight or draw attention to themselves unless they want attention, when such demands seem to be more directed towards the owners rather than other cats in the home. Tolerance of existing home sharers may be the norm, but any new cats need to be introduced carefully to the older cat. The protests of hissing and biffing may take some time to die down, far longer than one would expect in a younger cat.

Older cats will usually accept a kitten more readily than another adult cat. The kitten will not be so competitive and, even though there may be more pestering for play, the older cat can usually keep the upper paw on a young rapscallion. Clearly, one should carefully consider what the effects of introducing another cat (old or young) might be on an older cat. It must be acknowledged that this presents much more of a disruption than to a younger cat, which can actively work out a compromise, even if it doesn't want to be friendly. However, with the introduction of another old cat into a residence of elderly felines, tolerance will usually prevail if there are enough warm places for them all.

OUTDOORS

Outdoors most older cats seem less concerned with maintaining rights of access to a territory that they no longer wish to utilise and

131

are more content to let younger, local cats stake out their claim without protest.

To die with your boots on ...

However, if a cat has been the 'boss' cat of the neighbourhood, facing a loss of sovereignty can be hard to take, especially if some tough newcomer has moved in nearby. This can produce a more aggressive defence by the cat of at least the core to its old territory (around its home and garden) and lead to an increased willingness to expel any rivals that venture too close. It is a sort of back-to-the-wall defensive attitude that can get an old campaigner into a lot of trouble, and if the cat sustains physical injuries in the process then it may be time to manage its access to the outdoors more carefully to stop it getting into unnecessary fights. Wounds, physical and psychological, take longer to heal in old cats. A greater level of timidity at the unknown may also make older cats more territorial, perhaps because they are always on edge, trying to keep themselves prepared for the next encounter and tending to overreact to a perceived challenge.

... or hang up your guns

Other older cats see the loss of territorial control as part of the ageing process and accept their loss of control more gracefully. 'He has a reduced territory due to his greatly reduced level of activity and decreased motivation to hunt. Having given it up to other younger cats he never goes into the back garden now,' reported one careful observer on the behaviour of an old boy in his twilight years.

'Since he reached ten, he has avoided other cats,' said another cat owner, as if the cat had played it hard all the way until official retirement age.

Yet, as long as the old cat continues to go out on a regular basis, it is still likely to cling to some parts of its range and defend itself, at least to some level, if challenged, especially against life-long adversaries. Avoiding confrontations, if at all possible, but still putting up a good fight if it has to seems like the best policy for any older cat as long as it can defend itself. However, once old cats get beyond even self-defence, they are increasingly likely either to avoid all feline contact outdoors or to become more tolerant and appeasing, even friendly, with other cats, perhaps as much a tactic to avoid injury as a genuine new desire to be sociable. Many cats either choose not to go outside their own garden and patrol only their familiar territory and landmarks or simply watch the cut and thrust of territorial squabbles from the safety of a warm windowsill indoors.

GENERAL BEHAVIOUR CHANGES?

It seems that there is no general trend in the changes in behaviour associated with age in cats. It all depends, as ever, on the character of the cat. Some become grumpier, others more tolerant; many are more friendly towards their owners, other people and other cats, both indoors or out. There seems no way of knowing what is likely to happen until your cat starts to enter old age. But if 'patience' is what we all need to get the best out of relations with any of our ageing cats, other words often associated with the character of old people apply equally to some old cats.

The word 'cantankerous' rang true for some of the more negative comments made by owners who were clearly suffering from keeping their cat into its dotage. Nevertheless, most of them were resigned to waiting for the feline grim reaper to relieve their distress, and they

133

were not suffering enough to push them into taking a premature step. 'He doesn't like late nights and won't go to bed on his own … feels he has the God-given right to special treatment,' said the department of smouldering resentment in one cat-owning household, clearly glad of the chance to have a good moan when everyone else was being gushingly sympathetic about the cat because of its age.

And there is no hiding the joy in the pen of the writer who, when the good Lord finally ushered her old crumbly cat to the great mousing grounds in the sky, declared, 'I was delighted when a grumpy old cat I had homed for eleven months had to be put down. It was tails up all round for me and my other cats!'

DO PETS GRIEVE?

For most owners of older cats, however, part of the sadness of their old age is the knowledge that their pets could pass on at any time. While our cats probably have no forward concept of either their own mortality or that of their companions, they too may have to face the problems of bereavement when they lose a friend. In the Old Cat Survey, 102 (57 per cent) cats had outlived other cats in their household, though of these only 49 (27 per cent) had been companionable with any of their housemates. None the less, of the rest, 41 (23 per cent) demonstrated obvious signs of grief at the death of at least one of the other cats that they had known.

Their grief was expressed in a variety of ways. Some cried out or called more than usual in the days immediately following the death; others actively searched the house and favourite old resting areas for their friend; while a few even refused to eat for several days, one to such an extent that it had to be force-fed by its owners. Bereaved cats can become more noticeably friendly towards their owners, and for some the loss of their feline companion is the trigger for them to become very dependent on their human companions with the same attention-demanding behaviours as those described in chapter 6.

MAKING IT BETTER

Often owners introduce a new kitten or cat shortly after losing a pet in the hope that the surviving older cat will bond with it: 'He [a Burmese] was inconsolable for several days and nearly died. We got a new Siamese kitten, and they became immediate companions,' was the happy tale we were sent by one owner of a grieving cat. However, as cats are always so highly individual, this can often be something of a hit or miss affair. Breeds such as Siamese and Burmese do seem to form extremely close bonds once friendly with other cats in the home and certainly often with other littermates. While this can mean a much greater chance of serious problems when they lose a companion, it does mean that the acquisition of a new kitten is more likely to transfer their grief into something positive than it would with, say, a friendly moggy, for whom bereavement management can often be more difficult.

Although many older cats will pick themselves up from the depths of depression when presented with a new kitten, this could also be something of a nightmare for them. It may be fairer to get two kittens instead as they will be more likely to play their boisterous games with each other and burn off energy rather than focus all their social demands on the old cat. Yet, they will still interact sufficiently to keep the ageing cat happily and therapeutically occupied.

THE INCONSOLABLE CAT

Some cats have even pined to death after the loss of a close friend, when nothing – neither the introduction of a new cat or kitten, nor a change of environment, nor heaps of care and affection from the owner and the prescription of mild sedatives or alternative treatments from the vet – has been able to halt the psychological slide. But, while reactions of this scale may be rare, many cats do pass through some of the same grieving processes that we do when faced with the loss of a close friend or family member. 'When her friend died, she searched all the cupboards and got very depressed and confused,' was a typical description of a case that time would eventually heal -though we can never tell how long it takes for a cat to forget, or if it ever does.

Owners reported a wide range of reactions by their cat to the loss of another cat in the house. 'She woke up and sought attention from us at night for several weeks' was a typical response to upset by the older cat. The fact that the bereaved cat also 'wanted more cuddles and conversation' was equally understandable in an animal, which now more than ever needed new outlets for its sociability and looked to others for solace. 'The remaining cat became more sociable with everyone and all the other animals when the other cat died' was a description by one owner, but neither this nor the comment 'He became more attached to our dog' was so remarkable in an older cat that was used to a multi-species household.

CROSS-GRIEVING

'Fluff was quite lost without a dog to torment' puts the claw on the other foot, so to speak. It reminds us that dogs can also be driven mad or perhaps even to an early grave by the despotic behaviour of an old cat insistent on paying back, single-handedly before it dies, all the debts of dogs chasing cats in Tom and Jerry style. Another survey reply described how an older cat went into mourning after the death of a long-term companion, which many cats would normally have attacked and killed years earlier – a rabbit! But, whatever bad things happen to our old cats, including the loss of close friends, feline and non-feline, they resiliently try to get on with life, and time usually heals their distress.

A NEW LEASE OF LIFE

Some cats, perhaps having lived under a Pol Pot-style regime of terror for years, positively blossom at the loss of 'the other cat' from their lives and become much more rewarding as pets themselves. 'When our old Siamese died, our Burmese promptly assumed all her perks and became more sociable,' wrote one owner. Other seemingly less than charitable comments about the response of surviving cats to the loss of a feline cohabitee ranged from cats that 'seemed quite pleased when she died' to the joyful 'I think she celebrated' and the rather less than charitable 'He was delighted when the grumpy old bugger popped his clogs, and so were we!'

But most of us will be more than happy to nurse and care for our cats as they grow old and take account of their changing behaviour and demands. While physical needs may be easier to manage than in earlier times, psychologically it is all too important to remember to keep them stimulated and involved with family life to the level at which they are happy. Mrs Sarah Hartwell, a woman who specialises in looking after old cats, adds another careful reminder to us all in the light of her extensive experience. 'It can be easy to forget,' she says, 'to give the oldies individual attention as they are more in the background, and our younger cats are actively to-ing and fro-ing all the time,' but the more you put in, the more you and they will get out of life and each other.

8

Lap of Luxury

There are many benefits in having an older cat: most seem sedate, stable and more content than in their younger years; they know when to be around and when to keep out of the way; and they are in tune with the routine of the household. Often they are more demonstrative about showing their feelings, having built up a rapport with their owners, whereby the speaker and the listener understand each other's needs and secret codes. The gentle tap of a paw means a cuddle is urgently required, a loud mew means that the food bowl must be filled and sitting in a certain spot by the door means that help is needed with the cat flap. So just how can we respond to our older cat's needs and make its life comfortable?

HOW TO PAMPER YOUR OLDER PUSS

As we age our sleeping patterns change, and we tend to sleep less heavily but more frequently, as outlined in chapter 6. Older people often nod off in their chair by the fire or while watching television, yet do not sleep well during the night - our old cats are very similar. Someone in the Old Cat Survey commented of their oldie, 'He has generally slowed down, rarely climbs trees and watches more TV' – this could be true for any one of us!

WARMTH AND COMFORT

As outlined in chapter 1, normal body changes during old age mean that cats over the age of ten will begin to feel the cold more – they are less active and, because their coats may not be so thick or insulating, need to be kept warmer. Beds need to be situated out of draughts, preferably raised off the ground with high sides to protect from any cold breezes and to allow the cat to get cosy. Don't make the space too small as some older cats get stiff and so like to lie as flat as possible – they do not seem so able to curl up in a tight ball as they did in their youth. Always check the bed regularly to ensure it has not become damp or dirty as old cats are not so meticulous with their grooming and keeping themselves clean. Bacteria and fungi thrive in moist warm conditions and are just waiting for a weak animal with a less than efficient immune system to walk by.

If the cat has been out in the rain it may appreciate being towel-dried to remove most of the wet. Older cats have less oil in their fur, making the coat less resistant to water, which can penetrate between the hairs and down to the skin instead of just running off the surface. If the hair is matted or clumped it may even soak up water. We all know how the cold and damp make us feel achy and uncomfortable – add this to the likelihood that some old cats may have arthritis and aching bones and you will realise why most of them avoid the rain if at all possible. It may be useful to leave a shed door open or to have an old rabbit hutch filled with straw in the garden in case the cat cannot get into the house in time and needs to take refuge outside.

'He spends summer in the bath, winter on my chest' was the comment of one cat owner asked about her cat's sleeping habits. No doubt, just as old people dislike the cold long nights, cats too need comfort and warmth. Remember that, while you may be warm and cosy tucked under your duvet upstairs, the temperature downstairs may not rise above freezing, so a small radiator, or some other form of heat, in or near the cat's bed will be greatly appreciated. Warmth is a wonderful healer, and old cats also enjoy a heated pad (a metal pad that is heated up by plugging it into the mains and is available from most pet shops) or a hot water bottle inside a cover or wrapped in a towel – or even a luxurious sheepskin in their basket.

HOW TO MAKE YOUR BED …

Many cats also benefit from the tog rating of the duvet. It is estimated that about half of our pampered pet pussies sleep with their owners at night, some on the bed, some on the pillow and some lucky cats even under the duvet. But, for those pussies that don't go to the bedroom at night – as can be the case with very aged cats, which may be incontinent and therefore need a litter tray and easily cleanable floors around them – the position of their bed is important. Some may choose their own place, which may not seem to be the most obvious choice where warmth is concerned; however, they may have weighed the pros and cons of other spots and rejected them on security grounds. Rejected spots may be too near the ground and other cats or dogs or situated in a current of cold air, which we may not even notice.

In order to get away from danger or trouble they may try to find somewhere safe where it is possible to relax. So they may appreciate you placing a heated pad or beanbag at the site they have chosen rather than trying to coax them into a new position. However, most choose such obvious places as the airing cupboard, next to the wood-burning stove or, as our favourite Siamese used to, the little storage compartment in the bottom of the Aga – where it was warm enough to thaw a chicken, but not quite hot enough to cook a slow stew! Many cats like hammock-type beds, which hang on radiators, thus raising them away from the ground and any draughts, as well as allowing them to watch the activity of dogs or children from a safe height. Of course the main benefit is in being right next to the radiator. Here they will happily snooze away the day while watching what goes on around them – but woe betide anyone who lets the radiator go cold, when there are usually constant complaints until heat is restored.

... AND LIE IN IT

Hammock-type beds are especially comfortable because they suspend old bones rather than let them rub on hard surfaces. This is something to consider with bedding. A greater depth of cushions or blankets will protect protruding bones – a must for very old cats, who usually lose weight and so are more likely to be thin and bony and find it difficult to get in a comfortable position. Beanbags, especially the larger ones made for us human animals, are ideal as they allow the cat to spread out while still moulding to its body shape, giving all-round support and warmth. They are also very stable and unlikely to topple over.

Having chosen the bed and the best position, it is important to check whether your cat can reach it without trouble. It is all very well deciding that a high, out-of-the-way position is best so the cat can avoid the chaos of children, dogs and kittens, but how does it get up there? Make sure that there are easy steps up, and that the cat does not have to jump down and land with a sudden jolt on to hard ground. This can easily be done by using a pile of cushions arranged as steps or by suitably arranged stools and chairs, or you could make a wooden ramp (*see* diagram below) with a gradual slope, which can be raised and lowered to suit specific chairs, windowsills or tables. Covering the actual walkway of the ramp with carpet allows the cat to grip the surface and so avoid the possibility of slipping or slithering on bare wood. A made-up version of a ramp is on sale in the United States, where generally they seem to be most advanced in geriatric care, but, if you have a do-it-yourselfer in the house, making one of your own as shown in the diagram should not be too difficult. It is based on a deckchair design, so it can be raised or lowered as the height of the chair or bed demands.

CAT RAMP

The cat ramp is based on a modified deckchair design so it can be raised and lowered to various heights. The maximum height is 45-50 cm and width 30 cm. Putting carpet on the ramp enables the cat to grip easily.

A QUESTION OF BALANCE

Beds should be safe, stable and warm. Old cats appreciate some-where of their own where they can find refuge from the day's goings on or have a safe relaxed snooze. Perhaps if they choose the position you can make it cosy for them with padding and make it accessible by rearranging the furniture or adding a ramp.

Remember, too, that the old cat's balance may not be as stable as it was in its youth – it may still be amazingly good in human terms, but it may not be able to perform those gravity-defying feats of its younger years. Small ledges are best avoided as bed positions, and care taken to ensure that baskets can not rock off a ledge if the cat sits too near one side, or has suddenly to lunge for the edge as it climbs up.

A PLACE IN THE SUN

Often the cat's choice of resting-place in the daytime is on a sunny windowsill or in a chair in a shaft of sunlight. Don't underestimate the healing power and feeling of well-being to be gained from a snooze in the warm rays. One woman who specialises in giving homes to old cats remarked, 'Treat them as you do the washing – put them out in the sun and bring them in when it rains. In warm weather a cushion or folded blanket inside an open greenhouse is much appreciated by solar-powered geriatric cats.'

Warmth from the sun seems to have the ability to penetrate to the core of the cat's body and gently massage its aching joints. You can see the relaxation and pleasure in the cat's expression as it lies, usually flat out, soaking up the rays. An old sack or cushion in the cat's favourite sun spot in the garden would probably be greatly appreciated so it can bask in comfort.

A word of caution here though. Cats with white ears and pink noses may suffer sunburn because the hair does not protect the pink skin beneath. Continued exposure to ultraviolet rays over several years seems to have a cumulative effect and may lead to skin cancer on the ears or nose, so care from kittenhood is necessary for such cats. It may be better to keep them indoors during the middle of the day when the sun is at its hottest and to keep checking skin on the ears and nose for any signs of change. Older cats may sleep in the same spot for a long time, so owners should watch out for sunburn and check their pets regularly.

Of course, in the United Kingdom, it is not often that we have cause to worry about our cats becoming overheated. In hot countries, however, old cats will appreciate some form of cooling or air-conditioning as their tolerance of heat is also reduced with age. Taking old animals in the car on hot days is also best avoided – they will not be able to tolerate the excesses of temperature, which can arise, and they may become very stressed.

KEEP YOUNG AND BEAUTIFUL

Grooming is one of the cat's most important behaviours; not only is it important for keeping the coat in prime condition, but it also plays a large part in its social repertoire. Cats can spend up to one-third of their waking time attending to their coats. Grooming and washing not only ensure the hair is kept clean and free from tats – and is therefore a very efficient defence against cold or wet – but also help cats to create a group smell by grooming each other and by marking their environment with their own smell as they rub past furniture, other cats and their owners. This group smell is reassuring to cats and enables them to relax, secure in the knowledge that everything in their home is in the right place.

LETTING THEMSELVES GO

As cats age, they may become less efficient at grooming (this could also be caused by teeth problems, so check your cat's mouth if it stops grooming), and they are less supple at bending round to get to those difficult places. Very old cats may give up grooming altogether, and this is where owner attention is so important. Cats are known as meticulous animals, and a dirty cat is probably not very happy – we all know how awful we feel when our hair is tatted or we are in need of a bath, especially if we are feeling under the weather.

Owners of very old cats not able to groom themselves may well have to take over the task for them, if only in such a rudimentary manner as removing bits caught in the coat and gently grooming out old hair, which must make the cat feel both itchy and uncomfortable. Grooming not only allows you to check the cat's skin for any cuts, bites or parasites, such as fleas, lice or mites, but it also allows you to feel the outline of its body and notice if there are any dramatic changes or lumps and bumps, which are being obscured by its hair.

Grooming also spreads the oils produced by the glands on the skin and so helps maintain the coat's water resistance, and it probably relieves a few itches too. If the older cat is in a multi-cat household and gets on well with the other cats, it may be kept neat and tidy by its feline friends helping it groom around its head and ears. Many cats that would not tolerate being groomed in their early years seem to know you are trying to help them, and they enjoy the attention. Others may get very grouchy, perhaps because they feel a little fragile, so try combing little and often, giving lots of praise and cuddles, and you may gradually remove the tats.

EXTRA ATTENTION FOR LONG-HAIRS

A grooming glove or brush may be all that is necessary for the short-haired cat, but long-haired cats need considerably more attention. Without constant care, that previously luscious coat, which was once a pride and joy, can become knotted, rather smelly and look a real mess. Remember also that long-hairs have more risk of hair balls developing in their stomach and causing illness.

It may be necessary, therefore, to clip the coat if it cannot be kept under control, especially under the tail so that it does not become soiled and smelly, which would be unpleasant for the cat as well as for cohabitees. Large mats of hair may also be uncomfortable to lie on, and if they build up under the cats 'arms' they may make walking difficult. Clumps of hair are also ideal for trapping grass seeds in the summer, and these can actually begin to work their way into the skin and cause abscesses or even work their way into the body. The last thing an old cat needs is a general anaesthetic at the veterinary surgery so that the vet can clip its hair short all over because it has got beyond the stage at which a comb is of any use whatsoever.

CLAWS, GUMS AND BUMS

Regular grooming will enable you to check the cat's eyes and ears and to lift up its lips to look at its gums. Some cats appreciate a wipe with a soft cloth and warm water to clean eyes and the anal region (avoid using soap as this may cause irritation). It is also a time to look at the length of the claws and to clip them if they have become overgrown through lack of use. Long claws can, in the worst scenario, actually grow round and back into the pads, but even marginally long nails can get caught in cushions or the carpet. Old cats seem to have trouble retracting their more brittle claws as fully as they did when they were young, perhaps because the elasticity of the muscles and tendons holding them in place has decreased, and the claws tend to remain slightly unsheathed.

INS AND OUTS

While the older cat is less likely to keep coming in and out and banging the cat flap every five minutes – an art so well perfected by the feline youngsters of the household – it may forgo trying to use it at all because of problems of which you are unaware. While it has used the flap all its life without trouble, it now waits until the door or window is open before venturing outside, or waits to be called in through the open door before coming indoors. This may well be the time to check the flap: is it stiff, or has a new draught-proof one been installed, which the oldster cannot actually push open without a struggle? Does it snap shut on its tail before the cat has struggled through? Is the step up to it too high or the jump down outside just too much? All of these could be factors in the cat's reluctance to use the 'convenience'.

In winter, remember that the flap may become iced up, which is fine if you're stuck in, but being stranded outside in low temperatures can be dangerous for the older cat, which is not so efficient at maintaining its body temperature. It may be worth tying the flap open with a piece of string in the warm weather so the cat can enter and leave with ease, or replacing it with a piece of lighter carpet or plastic. Old cats will probably be very unwilling to learn to use a cat flap for the first time in their later years – even if you have installed it because they can no longer leap up to the window to get in. You may simply have to make steps up to the window instead.

Senile cats may have trouble with their sense of direction and stray around the neighbourhood, usually within close range of home but clearly lost and unable to find their way home. This is when it is important to ensure that the cat is wearing a collar bearing its name and phone number, so that neighbours can help out if they come across the disorientated creature. Many such owners pre-warn their neighbours of their cat's problems or post a card through the doors in their street just in case the cat turns up there. Putting a small but noisy bell on the cat's collar will also help you to pinpoint its position if it is wandering in the garden.

SAFETY OUTDOORS ... AND IN

Because of increased dangers outdoors combined with a cat less able to take avoiding action or to cope with change, some owners actually make their garden, or part of it, into a pen. The cat can then be out in the fresh air without worrying about wandering off or getting into danger. The construction should be of a strong wire mesh over a solid wooden or metal frame, and it should be sheltered from the wind. It must also offer shade for the animal in hot weather. It is useful to have grass and concrete areas with direct access from the house via a cat flap, and the enclosure should house shelves for sunning as well as tree branches or trunks for climbing and claw sharpening.

There are also hazards for the old cat in the house. Attracted to a window by that most irresistible of sounds, a buzzing fly, an old cat may not be so able to keep its balance; thus open windows can be a risk, as can the old route the cat has taken for many years up and over the roof and in through a bedroom window. Putting strong mosquito-net mesh over the window will enable it to be opened without the danger of the cat falling out.

GOING AWAY

One dilemma, which faces both dog and cat owners, is what to do with their animals when they go on holiday. Some people, worried that their cat will pine or become ill if it goes into a cattery while they are away, simply decide to stay at home. But will an older cat really be upset by having to go into a cattery? The answer very much depends, as do most things feline, on the individual personality of the cat and its ability to cope with change or stress. Certainly, change is more difficult for older animals to cope with, just as it is for older people. However, if the cat has been using a local cattery for many years and knows the people and the routine there, then it may not be overly stressed by the change of venue and will settle down happily under its hot lamp or on its heated bed and watch proceedings with a seasoned eye.

APPROVED CATTERIES

Putting an old cat into a cattery for the first time late in its life, however, may prove stressful. The worry can be greatly decreased if you know that the cattery itself is clean, efficient and caring of its residents. Good catteries are often found by word of mouth, but if you have no recommendations then go along yourself and have a look around. If the people in charge do not want you to see beyond the reception area, assume they have something to hide, then go home and choose another cattery to inspect. The Feline Advisory Bureau (FAB) produces a List of Catteries (*see* p. 179 for contact details) that pass its rigid standards for construction, care and attention for each cat. The list will help you to decide where to look, and you will notice the high standards that FAB listing demands.

Owners of such listed catteries have usually undergone courses in cat care, husbandry, identification of illness, business management and so on, so you can rest more easily knowing that any cat with special needs, such as the older cat, will be well cared for by them.

Such catteries will take extra care of an oldie and ensure that the heating is left on, and special diets or medication are catered for as necessary. Of course, it is up to the owner to ensure that specific instructions are given in writing, and that the name and address of the cat's vet are enclosed, along with permission for the cattery owner to request veterinary help if necessary.

EAST, WEST, HOME'S BEST

Most cats would undoubtedly prefer to stay at home when you go away, so if you are only absent for a short time, such as a weekend or a couple of days, and have friendly and trustworthy neighbours, it may be worth asking them to pop in, feed the cat and quickly check it over. However, if there are no such reliable friends nearby and you really do not want to put the cat into a cattery, or can not find a good one in your area, it may be worthwhile seeking out a reputable cat sitter who will come to your home and look after the cat's every need there.

Naturally such services are more expensive than a cattery, but they allow for the sitter to visit the home usually twice daily, to provide food and water, clean the litter trays, groom, play or just cuddle the cat and give it some attention. This may be all the old cat needs – it may simply snooze the hours away quite happily. The obvious worry about letting strangers into the house is that of security, and it is best to use someone who has been recommended because of a job well done elsewhere. Many sitters are aware of owners' concerns and are only too happy to supply references. Good service usually spreads by word of mouth.

MOVING HOUSE

Moving house is a potentially traumatic time for an older cat, which is set into its routines and lifestyle and bonded strongly to its territory. It may be worth putting a particularly nervous individual into a cattery or leaving it with a neighbour for a day or two while everything is being packed up before the move. Alternatively, leave it undisturbed in one room and pack that room last of all when the cat has been put safely into a travelling basket, so disruption is as minimal as the circumstances allow. Obviously with lots of strange people walking in and out carrying furniture and boxes, the move is going to be fairly frightening, and the cat may simply go and hide somewhere. This is fine as long as it can be found for the actual move. At the new home, it is best to keep the cat in one room until everything is sorted out and then to allow it to explore slowly, perhaps one room at a time, so that it is not overwhelmed by the unfamiliar territory. It can become secure in stages, as it becomes accustomed to the new smells, sights and sounds of each part of the house. Keep the cat in for a couple of weeks until it learns that this is now home, and to ensure that it does not wander off in search of its old stamping grounds.

Accompany the cat on its first ventures outside. Make certain it can get back in again easily as it will no doubt meet the neighbourhood moggies, which will try to chase off this new intruder into what they may see as their territory. Most old cats try not to cause trouble and will keep out of the way once they know what best to avoid. However, the first week or two can be a bit traumatic, so don't lock the old cat outside for too long and ensure it has a safe refuge. Squirting an intruding cat with water from a toy water-pistol can help to scare it off harmlessly, giving your cat time to make its new territory its own.

COMPETITION

If the older cat lives in a household with other felines or canines, it may need a little more individual attention than it did in the past. It is all too easy to cater for the brash young ones that push in to get to the dinner dish first, or are able to nip on to an empty lap before the oldies have gathered their strength to jump. Try to give old cats some special time on their own – when you are having elevenses or watching television in the evening, perhaps – and shut the youngsters out to have a cuddle or chat. Ensure, too, that the oldie is getting adequate food, if there is communal feeding. In fact, it may be better to feed separately so that you can see exactly how much is disappearing from the dish. This way you can monitor the cat's appetite and be alerted, if it changes suddenly, that there may be cause for concern.

COPING WITH PHYSICAL PROBLEMS

Many people are shocked when their vet tells them that their cat is going blind or deaf or will have to have a limb or tail removed. They worry about their pet's well-being, about how it will manage and if they can cope with it. Some owners decide that they do not wish their animal the trauma of an operation, or they realise that they cannot give it the attention it will need with a disability.

BLINDNESS

However, those who make the decision to keep their cat and help it through its problems often find that their pet copes remarkably well and can live an almost normal life with a little help from them. Take as examples the letters below, one from a woman whose cat went blind at about seven years old, and another about a very old moggie called Woden who went blind in his later years.

My cat is completely blind. In spite of this she settles down happily wherever we live and is content to live almost entirely indoors except for joining me in the garden sunbathing. She has also become deaf but shows no signs of frustration or distress over her disabilities except for the occasional 'shout' for help when she becomes disorientated. Human contact has become of the utmost importance to her. Our three dogs instinctively give her a wide berth and treat her with respect. I find living with a blind cat presents no special difficulties and, indeed, is a rewarding experience. She can be left alone for much the same periods as any housebound cat without any fears for her safety.

Annemarie Bishop

Until a few months ago I had a delightful elderly cat that came to live with me when his 'caring' owner dumped him by a main road. Woden was totally blind but mastered his new environment in a matter of weeks, going in and out of the garden and never failing to find his way up to my bed at night. It was interesting to see how my other six cats – usually selfish creatures – reacted to him. They seemed to sense his disability and never complained if he barged into them or trod on them as they sunbathed on the patio. As with a blind person, one had to be careful not to alter the position of the furniture and guests soon became accustomed to me yelling at them to pick up handbags and pull their feet up when lounging on the settee. It was a privilege to share our lives with Woden who brought us so much joy, in spite of his blindness, heart trouble and kidney problems. Whatever else was wrong with him, he was the champion purrer in our household and we miss him greatly.

Heather Smith

Blind cats do seem to be able to pick up the pieces and go about their lives with relatively few problems. Blind people will tell you that their senses of hearing, touch and smell become more sensitive, and that they rely on these other senses much more than fully sighted people. No doubt, the same is true for cats, and they enjoy the added benefit of having an amazing sense of hearing, a fantastic sense of smell and an ability to sense their surroundings by using their whiskers. They are also able to feel minute vibrations through their feet, so they are well armed to compensate for their lack of sight.

A fully sighted cat has very good eyesight and can pick up even the tiniest movement in the world around it. It can also see about six times better in twilight than us humans. However, cats do move about quite easily on very dark nights and in houses with little light. The whiskers on their face and elbows envelop them in a type of force field of sensitivity, and they can feel the slightest breeze in the movement of the air around them. Thus, they are able to feel their way through a very dark tunnel, simply by using their whiskers. A blind or partially sighted cat may move its head from side to side when walking along, using its whiskers as minesweepers or the equivalent of a blind person's white stick to help it negotiate gaps and avoid obstacles. It is vitally important that a blind cat should keep its whiskers – some owners have cats that like to chew off their feline friend's whiskers, which is not a useful habit for the blind cat.

A blind cat, just like a blind person, gets to know its way around the furniture in the house or the trees in the garden, so it is best to try and keep everything in the same place so it does not have to relearn the route each time. Remember, too, that a blind cat will rely more on its sense of smell than before, so it is necessary to be aware of how changing smells will affect it. Compared to the cat, man has a very poor sense of smell indeed, but it is simply a case of using your imagination to realise that a new carpet could completely disorientate the blind animal for a few days – its strong smell may overwhelm the familiar smells of the furnishings along the routes it usually takes. The cat will have a smell profile of its home, just as we would have a visual plan of our house in our minds. Change this by moving furniture around and you will not only affect the cat physically but may disorientate it mentally by altering this olfactory plan.

Using its senses of touch and hearing, a blind cat can follow a toy along the ground and play, and it can even hunt successfully. Onlookers would not guess the cat's handicap until the toy is lifted off the ground, when the animal immediately loses its ability to chase because, in the air, the toy causes no vibrations, friction or tiny sounds with which it accurately determines the object's position. By using this acute hearing and by feeling with its whiskers, when in close range, the blind cat overcomes its visual disability quite well.

Your presence will also be very important to the blind cat. It will hear and smell you and will learn to pinpoint you by your voice – so don't let the fact that your cat cannot see you keep you from talking to it. Conversely, putting a bell on the cat's collar, as suggested earlier, will help you to pinpoint the cat. A little thought and some simple rules and props will enable you and the cat to form a routine that allows a normal life. Visitors may be surprised to learn that the cat has a disability at all.

DEAFNESS

The same can be said for the deaf cat – in fact, many owners are very surprised to find that their cat has lost its sense of hearing because it can be a gradual process, through which the cat has compensated over the years and with which it copes well. Owners may have felt a little put out that the cat does not come when it is called or wake from sleep when they enter the room, but over the years they have probably attributed this to stubbornness or laziness.

As with the blind cat, the remaining senses become more acute to compensate for the loss of one of them, and, as we have said already, a cat can hear with its feet, picking up minute vibrations. If deaf humans can become concert musicians, then the cat with its very acute senses must be able to cope. A partially deaf cat can be warned or called by a sharp handclap, which it may be able to hear or even to feel the vibration in the air.

Some cats stop making any noise when they go deaf, while others do the opposite and keep up a continual stream of mewing, which can drive their owners to distraction. Because it is so difficult to know if a cat is deaf, it may help to write 'I AM DEAF' on its collar, where neighbours can easily see it and understand the need for care when it is sunbathing on their drive, and they wish to get the car out. It is also wise to check under vehicles before driving off. Have a little care for the cat's nerves, too – avoid frightening it by waking it suddenly from behind where it cannot see you. The letter below illustrates how well deaf cats can get on with life.

Puss was over eighteen when she was brought to the sanctuary. Her owner had a two-year contract abroad. He could not find anyone to take on Puss, nor could he bear to have her put down. After a few weeks I decided she would have to come home with me, and a temporary pen was prepared for her in the sitting-room. It was then that I realised that she was completely deaf. Her owner, with whom

I kept in touch, did not know this, as she must have adjusted gradually to her hearing loss. This also explained her detachment while at the sanctuary.

I knew that as my home was a completely new environment I would need to know exactly where she was because she wouldn't be able to hear me calling her. I solved the problem by attaching a bell – the type that budgies have in their cages – to her collar. Although she did not wander far, only going for a saunter upstairs or checking on the boundaries of the garden, the bell was most useful. A slow clank-clank meant that she was on an outward journey, a rapid clankity-clank meant she was homeward bound.

Because of her deafness she was inclined to be 'ratty'. She coped with the other cats by putting in her pennyworth first. A few choice words and a flick of the tail, as befits a grande dame, could soon put the others in their place. I always spoke to Puss in the hope that she would 'feel' the soothing words through my hands. Gradually she got to trust me and would allow me to spend an hour or so sorting out her long matted coat.

Puss lived with me for fourteen months. She died soon after reaching her twentieth birthday. Over the weeks, she had lost interest in food and life. She could not even be bothered to put the pesky kitten in her place. Those who knew her came to love and admire the way she adjusted to the closing months of her life. I have taken in a number of geriatric cats and never cease to be amazed how adaptable they are.

Elizabeth Mallison

AMPUTATION

To us the loss of a limb is a major disability and would seriously affect our lifestyle. Cats, with their amazing sense of balance, seem to do very well after the amputation of either a leg or the tail. Most adapt to being able to live their lives as normal cats, hunting, climbing and playing without any trouble – as the following letter illustrates.

I am a veterinary nurse and often come upon courageous animals that have not only survived illness but flourished afterwards. Once such triumph was Magnus, a tabby tom. He was brought into the surgery, a sorry, pathetic bundle, after a woman had noticed him in her garden, very much the worse for wear.

He was obviously distressed and frightened, and on examination we found that one of his back legs was gangrenous – this could have been the result of injuries following a road accident.

He was operated on that afternoon, and the leg had to be amputated at the top of the femur, leaving a stump. He was given antibiotics and analgesics and put in a cage in a quiet room to recover. On checking him the following morning, he was found to be plaintively meowing and happily rubbing himself on the bars of the cage. On being offered food, he ate and cleaned the bowl with relish.

During the next few days he joined us for coffee breaks and soon became a firm favourite with all the staff. Magnus tried to jump on my lap but failed. But, it was obvious to us that here was a cat full of guts and determination – he finally managed this feat after three days. His stitches were removed ten days after the operation, and I decided, with some trepidation, to take Magnus home with me, to meet our boisterous dog, Bertie.

My worries were unfounded, Magnus entered the house, looked around and made himself comfortable in Bertie's bed. He has become a much loved member of our family and is now climbing trees and playing with the local cats. It's easy to forget he's not a normal four-legged cat, and I am proud to have a cat who shows such adaptability and courage – in our house, he is the boss.

Tracey Fisk

TLC: THE VITAL INGREDIENT

The wonders of veterinary science have enabled our cats to live longer and healthier lives, but the old cat is inevitably ill more often than it was in its youth, and nursing is vitally important to its desire to recover. Veterinary surgeons will tell you that, no matter how miraculous a job they may do in stitching or medicating, the cat's will to recover is determined to a great extent by the quality of nursing care it receives. The cat can be coaxed into wanting to live by large doses of good old-fashioned tender loving care, otherwise it may give up merely because it becomes depressed.

It is very hard to generalise about critical-care nursing of cats because their recovery can depend less on the miracles of science and more on its personality and quality of bonding with the owner. Any owner who has an ill cat can do a great deal to help it to pull through. If it feels relaxed in its environment and confident with the people around it, then it is much more likely to get better. Gentle talk and tending, keeping the animal warm and away from draughts, encouraging it to eat, helping it to its litter tray and generally reassuring it with touch can make the difference between life and death. Cats that survive serious illness often form very strong emotional bonds with their owners – perhaps they realise and appreciate the care and love that went into bringing them back to health.

Such care does not come without rewards. The more you talk to owners of older cats, the more benefits there seem to be in owning one. As one woman put it, 'Old cats are the tops, companionable and far less worry than scatty kittens. If I had space and money I'd have a house full of old cats and spoil them rotten.'

FEEDING TIPS FOR CATS THAT WON'T EAT

A vital part of TLC is feeding. A body which is fighting disease or trying to recover from an injury or operation will need the nutrients and energy to do so. The immune system, too, needs to stay strong to fight off infection. If the cat does not eat, its body will start to break down its own structure and this in itself can make the cat feel unwell. It becomes a vicious circle of not eating and not wanting to eat.

Pain, infection and inflammation can all contribute to loss of appetite and after the vet has dealt with the medical aspects with painkillers, antibiotics, medicines etc, it is up to owners to try and coax their cat to eat. Here are some tips:

- Warming food will increase the aromas coming from it and perhaps just tempt the cat to try some. You know yourself how food is unappealing when you have a cold and cannot taste or smell it well, so if the cat is suffering from flu or has nasal discharge then clean it up and help him to feel comfortable and more relaxed about eating.

- Choose something your cat would usually kill for to see if you can kick start him into eating again. This may not be something that you want to feed long term but might just get him interested. Avoid baby foods that contain onion powder as this can be toxic to cats.

- Give small portions that do not put the cat off eating. Remove what is left and try again later – this also keeps the food fresh and more aromatic. Little and often is a good way to start. If this makes him feel a bit better he may want to eat more; patience is required sometimes!

- Put time in with the patient; feed small bits of food by hand and give encouragement and praise. If the cat feels secure he may be more likely to eat.

- If all fails to tempt the cat ask your vet about appetite stimulants and use them in conjunction with the ideas above.

If these still do not do the job, then your vet may be able to provide energy-dense special prescription food which can be fed with a syringe. Syringe feeding needs to be done with care as there is a risk of food being inhaled into the lungs. These prescription foods can also be given for the cat to lap up or can be used in feeding tubes which are put in through the nose and into the oesophagus. Cats tolerate these tubes well and this more direct feeding may help them turn the corner in their fight against an illness. Another way of feeding is putting a tube directly into the stomach under anaesthetic so the cat can be fed this way. While it may sound drastic it can be very successful. Once the cat begins to eat itself, the tubes can be removed.

9

Letting Go
and Starting Over

Most people know their pets as friends and loved family members. With this bonding comes all the emotions of a relationship – love, companionship, concern over illness and a wish to nurture. All these things help us to feel happy and secure. Our cats may have lived closely with us for fifteen years or more, through family and house changes, highs and lows, and they will have provided stability through these fluctuating times. Where, in many cases, our traditional nuclear-family values and experiences have been lost, pets have filled the gap. A simple example of this is recounted by a woman who always signed her Christmas cards from her human family as well as her cat. When one year she forgot to put the cat on a couple of cards, her friends rang up to find out if it had died. Obviously, even outsiders visualise some family units as including the animals, too, so why should we be surprised at the strength of our attachments to them when they live with us? In fact, acquaintances often remember the pets' names in the family better than those of the children.

When a pet becomes ill, most loving owners do all in their power – never mind the time or money factors involved – to save its life or help it through illness. Even those who thought they would simply have the animal put to sleep when it became too ill become intensely involved in helping it to have as long a period of quality life as possible to the end. We never know the strength of these bonds until they are put to the test, and old age combined with illness is one such occasion.

CONSIDERING EUTHANASIA

Sometimes the answer to the question, 'How can I tell when I should have my cat put to sleep?' is obvious. But, when the health of a cat is gradually deteriorating due to some chronic condition, it can be extremely difficult to know where to draw the line. The diagnosis of a terminal condition, such as cancer or advanced kidney disease, does not necessarily mean that a cat should be put to sleep immediately. These days, much can be done with such conditions to give the cat a few more happy and pain-free months or even years of life. Of course, it is impossible for us to know what is going on inside the minds of our pets but, having known your cat as part of the family for many years, you will be familiar with its behaviour patterns. As we have seen earlier in this book, the lifestyle of an elderly cat will gradually slow down as it ages, and illness will further limit its ability to live a completely normal lifestyle. However, the crucial point to be decided is whether, on balance, your cat is still enjoying life. The following questions may help you to come to a decision:

- Has your cat ceased to enjoy its food?
- Has your cat stopped responding to you and your family?

- Is your cat vomiting repeatedly?
- Is your cat incontinent?
- Does your cat have severe difficulty in getting around the house?
- Does your cat show signs of pain or discomfort when handled, such as yowling or hissing?
- Is your cat having frequent convulsions?
- Has your cat recently lost its sight?

If the answer to one or more of these questions is 'yes', and your veterinary surgeon does not feel able to improve your cat's condition with treatment, then euthanasia should be seriously considered. Your vet is experienced in judging the longer-term outlook for your cat and should be able to offer you guidance, although at the end of the day you are the person in daily contact with the cat, and the decision has to be yours.

WHAT IS INVOLVED IN EUTHANASIA?

This is not a very happy question, but one that troubles many owners of elderly cats, and worrying about the unknown is so often worse than the actual event. You will be very upset when your cat is put to sleep, and on request most veterinary practices will make an effort to schedule an appointment when you can bring in your cat away from the hurly-burly of a busy surgery. You may wish to have the procedure conducted at home, although there is a strong argument in favour of taking your cat to the surgery where your vet can carry out the task in ideal conditions and with nursing staff to hand. Some owners wish to stay with their cats, which is something some vets encourage. They feel that the cat will be more relaxed with its owner close by, who in turn is often relieved to witness how quick and painless the procedure actually is.

If the recommendation to put your cat to sleep comes as a shock to you, you may want some time to consider the matter and to prepare your family. If the cat is in distress, then it is selfish to prolong its agony, but with many conditions it is possible for the vet to administer drugs to keep the cat comfortable for another day or two.

HOW IS IT DONE?

If you decide on euthanasia as the most humane choice for your cat, you may be asked to sign a form giving consent for it to be performed. It is almost always carried out by injection with an overdose of a barbiturate, a drug used as an anaesthetic in lower doses, and it is not unreasonable to assume that the sensation experienced by the cat is exactly the same as if an anaesthetic were being administered and it slips into sleep. The injection can be given intravenously, which means that hair is clipped from a small area on a front leg, and the cat is then held by a nurse while the drug is injected into a vein. In most elderly cats that are thin, it is possible to feel the internal parts so easily that the injection can be given straight into an organ such as a kidney. In either case, the only pain experienced is the slight discomfort of the needle prick, and the effect of the injection is very fast.

Loss of consciousness is usually immediate, and very soon the heart will cease to function. It is quite common for the cat to take a gasp or two a little while afterwards, and you may also notice some muscle-twitching. Many animals evacuate their bladder or bowel. Do not be distressed – all this is purely reflex and does not mean that the cat is still alive. When a cat is dead, the pupils of the eye will be widely dilated, and the cat will not blink if the surface of the eye is touched. The heart will stop beating, and respirations will cease. With a very nervous cat, it may be necessary for the vet to inject a sedative first and then give the final injection once this has taken effect.

A NATURAL DEATH?

Deciding on euthanasia is difficult, and afterwards many owners are troubled with guilt about whether or not they made the right decision. Allowing a cat to die naturally seems to offer an easy alternative, in the hope that the cat will just fade away peacefully in its sleep. Unfortunately, the end does not always come this way, and cats often experience considerable distress in their final hours, vomiting repeatedly, struggling for breath or having convulsions. When it is obvious that your cat is no longer enjoying life, and veterinary medicine can offer no more, it is kinder to take the decision to have your cat put to sleep and ensure that any suffering is avoided.

DECIDING ON A RESTING PLACE

The death of a pet, either naturally or by euthanasia, brings about a period of grief and confusion when decision-making can be very difficult. If the cat has been euthanased at the veterinary surgery, the staff there will offer to dispose of the body, removing the need for you to deal with it. Often you may just want to get out of the way quickly and have a good cry on your own, so you may accept their offer without considering other options – or you may feel embarrassed about asking your vet what they are. Then, afterwards, you may wish you had taken the body for burial in your garden or private cremation.

So, if you can face the prospect, planning ahead is a sensible idea, and the options that follow may help you to do this. Some people feel that once their cat is dead its body is of no consequence because its 'soul' or spirit has gone, leaving merely an empty vessel; others wish to give the body a dignified and respectful farewell, and this will be part of their grieving process. Other members of the family, especially the younger ones, may also want to have a say in the matter, and the procedure you decide on may also help them to come to terms with their pet's death.

LEAVING THE BODY WITH THE VET

Many people are too upset or even embarrassed to ask their vet what will happen to their cat's body after euthanasia. If you want to know, then ask, and if you want to do something different, then this is the time to make your requirements known. It sounds callous to say, but deceased pets that are put to sleep at veterinary surgeries are officially defined as 'clinical waste' and have to be disposed of in an approved manner. Basically, this means deep burial at a landfill site or incineration.

Nowadays, however, most veterinary surgeries arrange for pets to be cremated, as this is generally thought to be the most acceptable method. Do not be frightened to ask your vet about what happens to pets that are put to sleep at that particular surgery and about any special arrangements, such as individual cremation or burial, that can be made.

HOME BURIAL

Many people these days do not have access to a garden or a large enough space in which to bury their pets, so this option may not be a choice for them. However, it is more common for cats to be buried than dogs, probably because of their size, and if burial in the garden is possible, this may be very reassuring. Home burial may give rise to a combination of feelings. That the cat's presence is still close by may be of comfort, and the grave can also help to provide acceptance of loss, both as a visual reminder and a focus at which to mourn.

Home burial requires organisation: where should the body be put; help with digging the hole; marking the spot and so on. It provides something to do during this period of intense grief. It also enables you to tend to your animal for a little longer, with the need to nurture not cut and frustrated quite so abruptly. This can be especially helpful after a long period of close nursing for a serious illness, when your pet's need of you is suddenly gone, and you may feel useless and a failure.

CREMATION OR CASKET?

If you only have a tiny space available in the garden but still want to have your pet's remains there, it is possible to have your cat cremated and then to bury the ashes (cremation is discussed further on p.170). On the other hand, if you have a larger space and wish to put the body in a casket, there are several pet-cremation services available, which offer a range of caskets.

Burying a favourite toy with the cat or wrapping it in its well-loved blanket may also help when you place it in its final resting place. If there is a likelihood of other animals digging up the grave, ensure it is quite deep – three feet or so – and then cover it with slabs or stones, which can also be made to look attractive. If you want to have a headstone or plaque, then there are many available from pet crematoria or masonry firms – The Association of Private Pet Cemeteries (*see* pp 179) will be able to help. Often planting a rose, tree or shrub over the grave provides a beautiful memorial and seeing the plant grow and flourish somehow signals new life from old. There are hundreds of rose and other plant names that may be similar to that of your cat, its colour or favourite game, which can give special meaning to the plant over the grave.

A burial at home may help family members, especially children, to accept that their pet is gone and will not come back. The grave itself offers a spot where they can go and talk to the animal if they want and at which to direct their grief. It is a chance for the family to say goodbye, and for children to see that everyone is upset, yet to share in the grieving process rather than bottle up their feelings.

PET CEMETERIES

There are now pet cemeteries throughout the country, and they provide a facility for burial for owners without a garden. They also allow the burial-place to be permanent, so that house moves and such like do not matter, and the body has a permanent resting-place. For some people the traditional graveyard setting is what they want for their beloved pet.

Your vet will know if there is a pet cemetery near you and will be able to give you details. You may want to visit it to see if you like the layout of the graves and the landscape and to talk to the proprietors about the range of services available. The added benefits for those without transport are that the cemetery will often collect the body from the vet's, prepare the grave and help with the burial. This includes supplying a casket if you want and being able to choose from a range of available headstones.

There are some things to check out, however, if you do decide to use a pet cemetery.

- Look at the costs. Pet cemeteries do not come cheap
- Find out if there is an annual maintenance fee to pay in addition to payment for looking after the grave
- Check that the cemetery is built on consecrated ground. If not, there is always the risk that, if the company goes out of business, the land could be sold and used for something else
- Check, too, whether graves are permanent, or if they are cleared and reused after a certain number of years

CREMATION

Just as many people opt for cremation either because there is no space available for burial or simply because this is their wish, an increasing number of pets are cremated too. Cremation can be communal with several other pets, as often happens if the body is left at the veterinary surgery, or it can be a single event involving just your pet. Obviously, a single cremation will be more expensive, but some people are comforted to have their pet's ashes for burial themselves.

The crematorium may also collect the body from the vet's so that this upsetting task is spared the owners. There are a number of companies around the country that perform this task, so make sure you ask them how they function and what facilities they have available. Ask, for example, if you can bring a pet's body for cremation; you can be present at the cremation; you will get a certificate guaranteeing that your pet was individually cremated, and that the ashes you are given belong solely to your pet.

OBITUARIES AND PERSONAL REMINDERS

Many cat magazines have a page set aside for obituaries, and this can be a very comforting way of saying farewell to your cat, as well as a public acknowledgement of your love for it, and the gap it has now left in your life. It is also something to keep as a personal memorial along with items of the cat's life. Lots of people keep favourite toys, photographs (or have a portrait painted from a photograph – again many artists advertise in the cat magazines) or even keep fur or whiskers. These small items can be a comfort, so do not be tempted to throw away everything associated with your cat because you are feeling desolate with grief – you may regret not keeping some mementoes later on.

Some people decide to give a donation to an animal charity or to an area of veterinary research that is attempting to find a cure for the condition from which the cat died. In this way, they may feel that the memory of their animal will survive in a positive way in order perhaps to help cure future generations.

REACTIONS TO LOSS

It takes weeks, months or even years fully to come to terms with the death of a dearly loved cat. Neil Lyndon, a journalist writing in *The Times*, commented:

> *The worst thing about keeping animals is not that they make a monkey out of you while they live, but that they rip you up when they die. Cats go nobly to their end, but their owners go to pieces. This grieving doesn't get any easier to bear with age. The deaths of our dogs when I was a child did not touch me more than the end of the alley mog, which came in my fortieth year. When my wife's*

favourite cat was killed on the road outside our house, we were in
mourning for three days.

Many people see the loss of a pet as the end of a chapter in their lives, and their emotions often stir up memories of other losses, both human and animal. Some people need to have a day off work – and this may not be seen too sympathetically by some employers, especially those who have not suffered the same experience themselves. Some have to talk to their family doctor because they become depressed – perhaps because they have had no one with whom to discuss their feelings.

While everyone believes that what they feel is unique to them, and that nobody else could understand how deeply they are upset, there are, in fact, stages of mourning and grief. Bereaved pet owners may not experience all of these or even in this order, but everybody goes through some aspects of this mourning process after a loss. Stages can overlap, and it may take a long time to get through all five phases some people may get stuck at one or regress back to another during the grieving process.

SHOCK AND DISBELIEF

Even if a death is expected, it can still bring about feelings of shock and disbelief. These may also be brought on by the initial diagnosis of a terminal illness. You may feel as if you are in a dream, and that you are waiting to wake up to find that everything is fine. It is hard to take in what has happened, and this is often worse if the cat is lost suddenly and without warning – you expect it to walk in through the cat flap any minute or call for its dinner as usual.

Some people ask for a second opinion if their vet says that there is little hope for recovery – no doubt holding out hope for a different diagnosis. Most of us also react by crying, and small things may set us off sobbing, which may not even be associated with our cat, and serve to send us over the fragile edge of self-control. Psychologists tell us that it is good to cry and talk about the death, rather than to bottle our feelings up. If you have the body of your cat at home, you may just want to wrap it in its favourite blanket, sit with it and stroke it for a while, until you can take in what has happened. Many people are reluctant to use the words dead, death or killed because they cannot yet accept that their cat has gone – time does not heal, but it helps.

ANGER

When you have got over the initial shock of your pet's death you often feel angry. This anger can be directed at the veterinary surgeon, whom you may feel did not do enough (even though you know there was nothing more that could be done), or at yourself, for not noticing the problems earlier (even when there were no visible signs to pick up). You may even feel angry at the cat for dying and at other animals for being alive (although you would not want anyone else to be going through what you are feeling). As you see, anger may not be logical, and it may be helpful to see it not as a personal attack but rather as a common reaction to the situation.

If you blame yourself, perhaps because your cat got out and was involved in an accident, your guilt may be very intense. This guilt reflects a strong wish to undo the situation – a time when we wish, as Superman actually did, that you could turn back time and replay the situation to change its outcome. You go through what you were doing at the moment the accident happened, when you saw the cat for the last time, and what you could have done to stop the accident. You forget to think that, if you went through every moment of the day like this, you would be seeing an accident around every corner and closet the cat in a padded room, so that nothing at all could ever go wrong.

GUILT AND BARGAINING

If the cat has been given a very poor prognosis, and the vet has said there is no chance of a cure, we still may try to bargain our way out of the situation. Often we resort to higher authority and ask God to let the animal live in return for doing something that we do not particularly like or that may cost us a lot of money. Some people proceed with costly treatment, despite their awareness that it is unlikely to work.

DEEP SADNESS

In grief we often feel very depressed, as if we have a heavy weight on our chest. Sometimes, when we are distracted and momentarily forget about the death of our cat, we are reminded of it again by this low heavy feeling. It is usually a very physical experience.

Just how long this depression lasts usually depends on how close we have felt to a particular animal and on how long we have been together, but it is said to start a few hours after the pet dies and may reach a peak within two weeks. Obviously a cat that has been with you for over fifteen years is going to leave a huge hole in your life. Having someone to talk to who appreciates this feeling, perhaps another cat owner who has gone through the same thing, will help. It is much worse for people who have nobody in whom to confide or no one around who knows how they feel. Some non-pet owners may unknowingly wound by saying things like, 'It was just a cat, not a human. You'll get over it.' Little do they know that the feelings are just the same, and sometimes more intense, at the loss of a pet.

ACCEPTANCE

After a period of time – there is no set limit on this – we pass through the stages of shock, anger, guilt and the intense pain of depression. Time can heal, as the old adage goes, although it is hard to accept this in the days and weeks around the cat's death. We find that we are able to begin to look at pictures of our pet again, to touch its collar or toys and to speak its name without that hollow pang of grief. It may be now that we can begin to think about getting another cat and sit down to consider the pros and cons of this. It is important to realise, though, that we must see the new cat as a personality in its own right and not as a replacement for the previous one.

THE REFUGE OF THERAPY

In one survey of veterinary clients who had lost a pet, 15 per cent said they would not wish to have another one because the emotional pain of loss was too great. Perhaps they had not gone through the whole grieving process but had become stuck and thus not reached the point at which they could look back and smile at the good times. It would be a pity for such owners to deny themselves the opportunity to love, be loved and enjoy the companionship of a cat again. However, on the other hand, never be forced into getting a new cat or kitten if you do not feel ready for one.

If you find, though, that after a couple of months you still cannot cope with your grief, and you are suffering from depression, sleepless nights or headaches and can not get back into your normal routines, you should ask for help. A qualified counsellor will understand how you feel and help you to come to terms with your cat's death. A wonderful book entitled *Absent Friend* has recently been written by Laura and Martyn Lee. Martyn Lee is a veterinary surgeon, and Laura Lee has spent several years involved in bereavement counselling. It is a compelling read as well as a great comfort if you have lost a pet It is available price £5.45 (including p+p) from CPC, A505 Main Road, Thriplow Heath, nr Royston, Hertfordshire SG8 7RR. The Blue Cross animal charity has teamed up with the Society for Companion Animal Studies to provide a Bereavment Helpline and can be an excellent source of help. Call 0800 0966606.

STARTING AGAIN

Some people replace a lost cat with another one almost immediately, while others need to wait for some time until they are ready to accept a new character into their lives. You must realise that not only will the new cat be different but that you also will have changed since your previous cat was a kitten.

If you are getting a new kitten after the death of an aged cat, you will find quite a difference. Don't be tempted to make comparisons, simply enjoy the new character and all that exuberant energy and look forward to many years of companionship and love. Meantime, enjoy your ageing puss.

ON A CAT, AGEING

He blinks upon the hearth-rug
And yawns in deep content,
Accepting all the comforts
That Providence has sent.

Louder he purrs, and louder,
In one glad hymn of praise
For all the night's adventures,
For quiet, restful days.

Life will go on for ever,
With all that we can wish:
Warmth and the glad procession
Of fish and milk and fish.

Only – the thought disturbs him –
He's noticed once or twice,
The times are somehow breeding
A nimbler race of mice.

Alexander Gray

Appendix

FELINE ADVISORY BUREAU
Taeselbury
High Street
Tisbury
Wilts SP3 6LZ
Tel: 0870 742 2278
Fax: 01747 871872
e-mail information@fabcats.org
www.fabcats.org

ASSOCIATION OF PET BEHAVIOUR COUNSELLORS
PO Box 46
Worcester WR8 9YS
e-mail apbc@petcent.demon.co.uk
www.apbc.org.uk
Pet Bereavement Support Service
co-run by the Blue Cross and the Society for
Companion Animal Studies
0800 0966606
e-mail: pbssmail@bluecross.org.uk

ASSOCIATION OF PRIVATE PET CEMETERIES
AND CREMATORIA
Nunclose
Armathwaite
Carlisle
CA4 9JT
www.appcc.org.uk
e-mail: contact@appcc.co.uk